Praise for *Mastering Collaboration*

Mastering Collaboration makes a clear and compelling case that collaboration is not just a squishy 'nice to have,' but rather a mission-critical skill for modern organizations. Even better, it provides actionable strategies and tools that you can begin using right away to improve the way you communicate and collaborate with your colleagues.

—*Matt LeMay, author of* Agile for Everybody *and* Product Management in Practice

While feted as the foundational value of every innovative knowledge industry team, high-quality collaboration is a remarkably under-studied phenomenon. In this book, Gretchen Anderson finally breaks that pattern. She identifies and then explodes common myths that many teams hold about how collaboration really happens, and then explains how we can work together even more effectively to build stronger, more effective teams.

—*Blair Reeves, coauthor of* Building Products for the Enterprise

T0319418

Mastering Collaboration

*Make Working Together Less Painful and
More Productive*

Gretchen Anderson

Beijing · Boston · Farnham · Sebastopol · Tokyo

Mastering Collaboration

by Gretchen Anderson

Published by O'Reilly Media, Inc., 1005 Gravenstein Highway North, Sebastopol, CA 95472.

O'Reilly books may be purchased for educational, business, or sales promotional use. Online editions are also available for most titles (*http://oreilly.com*). For more information, contact our corporate/institutional sales department: 800-998-9938 or *corporate@oreilly.com*.

Acquisitions Editor: Melissa Duffield	**Indexer:** Ellen Troutman-Zaig
Development Editor: Angela Rufino	**Interior Designer:** Monica Kamsvaag
Production Editor: Christopher Faucher	**Cover Designer:** Randy Comer
Copyeditor: Rachel Monaghan	**Illustrator:** Rebecca Demarest
Proofreader: Kim Cofer	

March 2019:   First Edition

Revision History for the First Edition

2019-03-01:   First Release

See *http://oreilly.com/catalog/errata.csp?isbn=9781492041733* for release details.

The O'Reilly logo is a registered trademark of O'Reilly Media, Inc. *Mastering Collaboration*, the cover image, and related trade dress are trademarks of O'Reilly Media, Inc.

978-1-492-04173-3

[LSI]

Contents

Preface

It's Complicated: Our Love/Hate Relationship with Collaboration

Collaboration is a skill that many agree is crucial to deal with big, complex challenges where causes are unclear, and the knowledge and abilities required are diverse. We need to be able to harness the energy of lots of different kinds of people productively, without getting mired in conflict or hiding out on our own where we feel safe and in control. Collaborating well doesn't happen naturally; it requires an understanding of what helps teams come together, and how to avoid or push back on forces that get in the way.

Working closely with different types of people to solve difficult challenges is something we say we value. Many blog posts and advice columns praise the virtues of collaboration as critical to how we work now, and schools have begun teaching it as a critical skill for the 21st century. We know that we can't solve the complicated problems before us—from climate change to artificial intelligence to health care for our exploding population—with just a few people who think and act the same. When it goes well, collaboration brings out new ideas and joins varied skills to create something truly inspiring. But when it goes wrong, it drives us back into safe groups with defined rules where we can focus on something that's easier to control.

And it does go wrong, because the reality is that most people aren't taught how to work in a collaborative environment, with all of its messy interpersonal dynamics. What I've learned from studying and practicing collaboration in many different settings is that getting it right doesn't happen on its own. Often, "successful" outcomes are not very collaborative at all, but rather the result of someone spending hard-won political capital to drive a vision they care deeply about, whether others are on board initially or not. And at the end, it doesn't even feel much like a victory. There's no time to celebrate when they must now spend months rebuilding the relationships they called upon and shoring up their political capital for the next new idea campaign. It's exhausting!

When collaboration fails, it's almost a nonevent. Few teams actually come together and launch something absolutely, catastrophically bad. For the most part, collaborations simply dissolve and everyone goes back to the status quo, back to their silos, back to creating the safe, achievable Band-Aid solutions that are easiest to implement. Except most of those involved now have a bad taste in their mouths—for other teams, for leaders, and for collaboration itself.

The collaborations that go off the rails share some common elements, just as the successful ones do. In developing this book, I've spoken with people in many different fields to understand how they team up, what works, and what doesn't to help us get our arms around it. The insights I've gleaned from speaking with different types of collaborators—educators, product developers, aeronautics experts, ER doctors, and civil servants—can be applied widely to make collaboration less painful and more productive.

We need to get better at managing diverse groups of people working together, because working in silos that we can control won't get us where we need to go. Eventually, those Band-Aid solutions become unworkable; breakthroughs are needed. Sooner or later, the breakthrough will come, maybe from a team who just got lucky. But being able to come together to solve problems is too important to leave to luck. Getting different people to work together to solve complex problems that affect us all is a critical 21st-century skill that's worth mastering.

Why I Wrote This Book

My inspiration for writing this book was watching well-intentioned, capable leaders say all the right things about collaboration and teamwork, only to fumble when trying to pull it off. They express the need to get wider perspectives on initiatives, to improve cross-functional teamwork, to change their order-taking cultures, but in the end they reveal a predefined solution and ask, "Any questions?" Some leaders simply shove a team together into a conference room with a problem to solve and hope for the best. Or, they bring in outside consultants to make the magic happen, and it does, right up until it comes time to take the ideas back inside and it all falls apart. Leaders may think that they love collaboration, but many just don't know how to embrace it.

Because it's so important, getting "good" at collaboration can't require an overnight shift in the way an organization operates. I've witnessed, and interviewed others about, huge "transformation" efforts within large, established organizations where the natural environment isn't conducive (or is downright hostile) to working across silos that can be controlled independently. Attempting to change that environment wholesale is likely to fail since there are too many antibodies you have to contend with. Startups have an advantage in that they have less inertia in the culture and its approach to working together. But even these organizations can resort to just executing on known problems, deferring more complex questions until tomorrow when the company will be (hopefully) more stable, only to find themselves just as stuck when that day comes. Startups carry a level of pressure that favors independent action just as much as large companies.

Instead of trying to change an organization's whole culture, then, this book aims to arm you with knowledge and tools to succeed in a grassroots scenario where you can build acceptance of working differently by demonstrating results, not by selling a process, methodology, or value system. For those who lead or support efforts to bring people together to solve a problem, you should look to create a space within the organization where a team or teams can bring their diverse talents together, with the right support.

Who This Book Is For

This book is for anyone who needs to bring people together to diagnose problems and explore solutions—from product managers looking to get buy-in for product roadmaps, to engineering leaders looking to support development teams, to students learning to work in groups. Whether you're looking to support a large-scale initiative or just want some tips to reduce team friction, this book offers practical advice, guiding principles, and simple tactics that you can use to master collaboration.

How This Book Is Organized

This book breaks down four major aspects of how collaboration works and how you can support it. Each part contains advice, troubleshooting, and specific tools that you can use to support healthier working relationships that deliver great outcomes.

INTRODUCTION: WHAT'S COLLABORATION AND WHAT GETS IN THE WAY?

In this chapter, we'll look at what situations call for collaboration, and what makes it a challenge. In each of the four parts of the book you'll find guidance about how to overcome those challenges.

PART I: CREATING THE RIGHT ENVIRONMENT

Business settings can challenge collaboration because of the inherent power dynamics and typical workspaces. This part helps you adapt that environment to support healthy teamwork.

- Chapter 1, *Enlist Everyone*
- Chapter 2, *Give Everyone a Role*
- Chapter 3, *Enable Trust and Respect*
- Chapter 4, *Make Space*

PART II: SETTING CLEAR DIRECTION

Many collaborations fail because they lack the structure and focus they need for diverse teams to feel safe and be productive. This part looks at how you can provide the right structure for teams to manage their time, set expectations, and understand what success will look like.

- Chapter 5, *Make a Plan*
- Chapter 6, *Set Clear and Urgent Objectives*

PART III: EXPLORING SOLUTIONS

Teams need support to be open to new ideas and create solutions that blend different perspectives and skills. This part gives you tools to lead teams through creating and testing out ideas early and often.

- Chapter 7, *Explore Many Possibilities*
- Chapter 8, *Make Sound Decisions*

PART IV: COMMUNICATING CLEARLY

One challenge that plagues many collaborations is communicating with those who aren't intimately involved day-to-day so that they're well informed and able to provide useful guidance and feedback. This part will help you communicate clearly within the team and with others to keep the collaboration flowing and reduce friction.

- Chapter 9, *Find Out What Others Think*
- Chapter 10, *Communicate Transparently*
- Chapter 11, *Tell the Story*

Throughout the book, you'll also find sidebars that contain tactical exercises, tips, and techniques you can use with your team to improve various aspects of working together. If you and your teams can master these fundamentals and use some of the techniques provided, you'll be better equipped to tackle messy collaborations with grace and get the benefits your challenges require.

Acknowledgments

This book may only have one author's name on the cover, but it contains the insights and stories from many lovely people who were generous with their time and energy. I want to thank those who shared their experiences with me: Jimmy Chin, Jon Rosenberg, Christina Wodtke, John Simpkins, Jim Kalbach, Chad Jennings, Catherine Courage, Mikael Jorgenson, Michael Grasely, Kai Hayley, Vanessa Cho, Sara Ortloff, Alberto Villarreal, Paul Ford, Michael Sippey, Farai Madzima, Matt Bellis, Josh Seiden, Andrea Mangini, Brandon Harris, Adam Richardson, Kate Rutter, and Cyd Harrell.

To my reviewers, Greg Beato, Jorge Arango, Pilar Strutin-Belinoff, Jason Mesut, Matt LeMay, Blair Reeves, David Farkas, and Lane Goldstone, who helped me get from a mess of ideas in my head to something coherent and much improved, I hope that I may repay the favor someday. At the very least, you have paid it forward, friends.

To Susan Killebrew and Pam Lucker, who inspired me by showing me that collaboration wasn't just something you are born with but something you can teach, you are creating the collaborators of the future, who will likely face even more complex and important challenges. Thank god they have you. And thanks to both for turning me on to Elizabeth Cohen's *Designing Groupwork* (Teachers

College Press), a book that several educators say they use for teaching collaboration in the classroom.

A special shout-out to some of my past collaborators: I know working with me was not always easy, but hopefully it was worth it. I learned so much from each of you: Eric Bailey, Ben Foss, Ariel Waldman, Kim Goodwin, Mark Seveska, Nikki Lasley, Karissa Sparks, Jen Theaker, and Sharilyn Neidhardt. And to David Cronin, my ultimate collaborator.

O'Reilly Online Learning

O'REILLY® For almost 40 years, *O'Reilly* has provided technology and business training, knowledge, and insight to help companies succeed.

Our unique network of experts and innovators share their knowledge and expertise through books, articles, conferences, and our online learning platform. O'Reilly's online learning platform gives you on-demand access to live training courses, in-depth learning paths, interactive coding environments, and a vast collection of text and video from O'Reilly and 200+ other publishers. For more information, please visit *http://oreilly.com*.

How to Contact Us

Please address comments and questions concerning this book to the publisher:

O'Reilly Media, Inc.
1005 Gravenstein Highway North
Sebastopol, CA 95472
800-998-9938 (in the United States or Canada)
707-829-0515 (international or local)
707-829-0104 (fax)

We have a web page for this book, where we list errata, examples, and any additional information. You can access this page at *oreil.ly/mastering-collaboration*.

To comment or ask technical questions about this book, send email to *bookquestions@oreilly.com*. For more information about our books, courses, conferences, and news, see our website at *http://www.oreilly.com*.

Find us on Facebook: *http://facebook.com/oreilly*
Follow us on Twitter: *http://twitter.com/oreillymedia*
Watch us on YouTube: *http://www.youtube.com/oreillymedia*

Introduction

What Is Collaboration, and What Gets in the Way

If you want to go fast, go alone. If you want to go far, go together.

——UNKNOWN

The 21st century has brought our society great new capabilities, such as landing on Mars and editing genes to treat disease, but it has also brought us complicated, intractable problems like climate change. We need to get better at coming together to solve these problems, because no one person is going to make a dent on their own. But many people find collaboration difficult and exhausting compared to working in simple teams of like-minded individuals with clear lines of authority. In my own work, I have experienced the temptation to take a narrower, more isolated path. But even when it's difficult, the experience of working closely with someone who is very different is ultimately rewarding, and generates better answers. While not everyone is a natural collaborator, we can all adopt different behaviors and approaches to make working together better.

What's Collaboration? And What Isn't?

In researching this book, I've heard many people say that collaboration is simply "the air we breathe" and covers almost every aspect of our work. Kate Rutter, principal at Intelleto and author of *Build Better Products* (Rosenfeld Media), has a useful model for defining teamwork at several levels, which I have adopted (Figure P-1). She lays out the difference between cooperation, collaboration, and co-creation. At the most general level, Rutter says, is *cooperation*. Cooperation describes people doing things in a coordinated fashion, in a clear order, according to shared standards. She and I agree that while this is important, cooperation is very different from collaboration in that it describes work that is well under-stood and can be structured, sequenced, and monitored in a more straightfor-ward way.

At the other end of the spectrum lies *co-creation*, where two or three people are actually making something together. They've got their hands in the dirt, as it were, and apply skills to something tangible, whether it's a policy or a product. I will address this type of collaboration briefly, because there are techniques and methods you can employ for co-creation that will help you when you take their output to a wider group. Much has been written about how to do co-creation—from *Sprint* (*https://www.thesprintbook.com*) (Simon & Schuster) by Jake Knapp to "Pair Design" (*https://www.oreilly.com/ideas/pair-design*), which I wrote with Chris Noessel for O'Reilly—and you will find many ideas there to get better results.

Collaborate

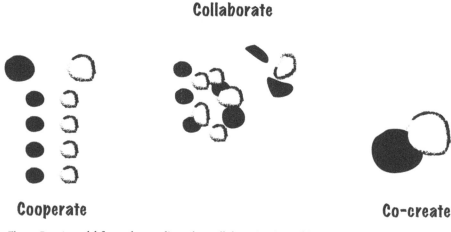

Cooperate   Co-create

Figure P-1. A model for understanding what collaboration is, and is not

Rutter says what lies between cooperation and co-creation is *collaboration*, where a diverse group of people are responsible for an outcome, but may not all be working hands-on to build the solution. This is where this book will mostly focus: how to get alignment of purpose, how to guide smart decisions, and how to broker politics that large diverse groups will inevitably face. Collaboration at this level often involves "fuzzy frontend" thinking where both the solution and the path to it are neither obvious nor planned. Collaboration may be messier and involve leveraging very different skills in nonlinear and unpredictable ways.

Collaboration doesn't come in one specific form, and doesn't follow a recipe. It might be a set of people who are working independently on a common problem, sharing their work early and often to get feedback and test out ideas. Or, it may be a team of people from different business functions who go offsite for a week to hash out a new compliance framework. Collaboration can be a group of developers, designers, analysts, and product managers developing a product or service, or even a set of teams working on parts of a product or service system that needs to be coherent to those who use it.

Choose the Right Problem and Moment

Collaboration can take many forms, but at the core it's a way to drive more innovative solutions to problems. Because it's challenging, we need to be careful not to start throwing "collaboration" at every cooperative situation, making things that should be straightforward into complex arguments, or inviting too many people into a co-creation space and slowing it down.

Collaboration is especially useful for addressing the following issues:

Taming complexity
First, we benefit from bringing diversity to a problem, whether it's diverse skill sets, cultural perspectives, or customers and employees. The ability to channel the experiences and skills of many people when solving a problem means you generate more potential solutions, and tests of those solutions, quickly.

Facing ambiguity
Collaboration is also incredibly useful when the challenge being faced has unknown unknowns, and there isn't a clear, structured path forward to find a solution. In these situations, collaborations, given the right space, can help a small group of trusted colleagues feel out the unknowns from different angles.

Getting alignment
Getting buy-in from large groups of stakeholders can also be improved by collaboration. When it's done right, stakeholders, given a chance to participate in creating the solution, will be more invested in its success.

Engaging employees
Companies spend a great deal of time and energy assessing and supporting engagement among employees. They know that workers who are intrinsically motivated and who have a sense of ownership over their work produce higher-quality work and have lower turnover rates. These employees are

the profile of 21st-century workers who can think nimbly and adapt to changes because they have resilient partnerships among colleagues. These are also employees who are better suited to solving complex problems versus executing known work patterns.

We'll cover each of these issues in more detail next.

TAMING COMPLEXITY

Paul Ford, a well-known serial, solo entrepreneur, recently founded his own studio, Postlight, helping clients realize new product concepts. "As you grow in the industry," he says, "you learn you can't do it all. Especially now, with tools as they are more robust, it's basically impossible for one person to ship a truly innovative product anymore. The tech stack is so vast, you need to be able to tap into everyone's strengths."

It's not just our tools that have gotten more robust and varied; the wicked problems we face have gnarled root causes demanding varied viewpoints and specialty skills. In his excellent TED talk, "When Ideas Have Sex" (*http://bit.ly/ 2EDomrP*), Matt Ridley points out that ideas are never just born *de novo* but are always an evolution sparked by someone else's ideas and solutions. He considers the creation of something as prosaic as the computer mouse and all of the intricacies involved in creating it. Even the most competent maker on earth couldn't single-handedly pull off creating one once you consider not just the making of circuit boards and buttons, but also the petroleum refinement needed to make the plastic and the firmware to control the interaction with the computer. We can and must stand on the shoulders of giants.

When problems have many intertwined causes, or solutions require novel skills and materials, it's critical to be able to bring a diverse group of people together to be productive.

FACING AMBIGUITY

Many teams do just fine with a well-understood problem where each person can cooperate and do their part. But when the challenge doesn't have a clear answer, people start to fear failure and doubt their ability to contribute. Collaboration helps us deal with the unknown by harnessing the diversity of skills and experiences in the team to test out ideas and mitigate risk. And the more diverse the team is, the better able they are to see ambiguity from many sides and create better understanding by using their various perspectives to shore up a fuller picture.

When you face unknowns or tackle something novel, you need to be able to blend the skills and perspectives of a group to avoid pitfalls that you can't see.

GETTING ALIGNMENT

It's tempting to think that what you need from teams and leaders is agreement. Josh Lovejoy, now Principal Design Manager at Microsoft, says he learned the hard way that "getting to yes" is a real trap, because when you ask for agreement, you may get it just so you will go away. True alignment requires time and space to air out differences and make sure that what we're agreeing to is more fleshed-out than a few bullet points or truisms. When we allow a group to wrestle appropriately with a problem, their mental pictures start to actually resemble each other and the friction they experience decreases. Even when alignment is difficult to achieve, the discussions around making decisions, provided they are healthy, can make the entire group smarter.

When decisions span many types of people, getting them to participate helps build a shared understanding of the situation and how to proceed.

ENGAGING EMPLOYEES

But collaboration isn't just about the ability to channel lots of different POVs and types of expertise. Reid Hoffman, the founder and executive chairman of LinkedIn, knows the value of healthy teams means more than just low turnover. He sees the trust between employees as a competitive advantage because they can deploy their expertise at faster and faster rates to get better solutions. His new book with Chris Yeh, *Blitzscaling* (HarperCollins), spells out this relationship in case studies across industries and differently sized organizations, where a key part of the answer is enabling engagement.

When an organization needs to build camaraderie and a sense of mission, supporting collaborative work gets people more deeply engaged. But there are forces at work in most business contexts that make collaboration something that doesn't happen simply by putting people together.

What Gets in the Way of Good Collaboration?

Collaboration isn't something that is easy to do. It goes against our human nature in some ways, and it conflicts with many aspects of corporate culture. Very often, what passes for collaboration is what I call "collaboration theatre," where people work side-by-side on the same problem without actually combining their talents. Sure, we get real people together in a room and ask them to write stuff on Post-its. We send out surveys to hear what our peers and employees think. But often all of that activity is really just masking the same old ways that companies always make decisions, where "experts decide" what's important, what's working, and who's right.

Tom Chi, a product development luminary, described his first day at what would become Google X at the Google Sprint Conference in October 2018. Chi was thrilled to join a team of brilliant people from all different backgrounds that had been assembled by Sergey Brin to work on the Google Glass concept, among others. During the first few hours of the day, the team began a debate over what color the display for the device should be. The color choice would have implications for what material would make up the surface of the display and how much power would be needed. After a hour of intense debate, the issue was decided. Brin, Google's founder and Silicon Valley genius, asserted that the color would be red. His rationale was clear: red photons have the lowest energy level, and thus would take the least power to project and would cast the least energy on the retina. Also? It's always red in sci-fi.

Chi, having just left Yahoo, found himself feeling uncomfortable. This kind of decision-making—from smart, senior people with no real evidence, only conjecture—was the kind of thing he wanted to leave in the past. So he advocated strongly that, before the team committed to that decision, they try something out. And they did. Within the first day they had a super-crude prototype that they could use to project a paragraph of text onto a display to see what worked. The results were unanimous. Red was the worst color, by a long shot.

The decision-making approach where one expert decides based on great assumptions is what Chi calls "guess-a-thons," and you've undoubtedly encountered them yourself. In a guess-a-thon, smart people have really smart reasons and confidence behind their guesses, which makes them seem indisputable. But as the team saw, there was a lot to dispute. As it turns out, Brin was right, in a way: red photons do have the lowest energy potential of the visible spectrum, which means when you try to focus on them out in the world or in a room, they become overpowered by every other color of light, making them impossible to read.

Collaboration theatre and expert-driven guess-a-thons set teams up to fail for all the right reasons. And the stronger the leader, the worse the effect, since they are trusted to use their talents and power to guarantee greatness for the team. But one person, no matter how powerful, can't drive people to a solution when the problem is complicated and ambiguous. Actually harnessing the power of many different people takes more than a strong leader; the team itself needs to be engaged and supported.

So what's going on that makes us resort to theatre instead of real collaboration? To master collaboration, it's worth understanding what gets in the way, specifically in a business context.

THE ENVIRONMENT FAVORS INDEPENDENCE AND INDIVIDUALISM

We talk about our teams at work, but in many ways, business is a solo sport. We are evaluated and rewarded individually. We often compete with peers for an ever-shrinking number of more valuable positions. This model carries perverse incentives for individuals to garner attention for themselves for work that was performed by a group. For managers, come performance review time, it can often seem like your employees were all carrying out 10 different, yet very similar, efforts that each succeeded because of one person's heroic efforts. Being independent is appealing because we are rewarded individually so it's easier to stick to a silo or a solo effort, rather than get into a situation we can't fully control.

The business context doesn't do much to help teams be open and trusting with each other, either. Teams are often assembled by outside management, with little attention paid to helping them overcome the interpersonal dynamics that come with bringing diverse perspectives together. The focus tends to be on a team's output, so we label those who show progress by any means necessary "high performing teams," without attending to whether the collaboration is actually healthy.

Our business environment also challenges teams to use space productively. Open office plans, originally designed to promote collaboration, turn out to have the opposite effect (*https://hbs.me/2GPqSAP*). Collaboration isn't something that is done face-to-face, side-by-side, 100% of the time. We need to find ways to give people some time away, as well as ways for teams to be effective even when members are remote.

The tools we use to collaborate can also be a challenge if they are too constricting or too chaotic. Teams can hide behind tools that are meant to support open communication. We send an email or a Slack message rather than have a face-to-face or even phone conversation where we might work through issues more efficiently and entertain more complex ideas.

To make the conditions for collaboration supportive, we can focus on who we include, and how, to make sure a team develops the trust needed to bridge gaps and have breakthroughs. We can also set up their space and tools such that they enhance the team's ability to build a shared understanding and vision.

WE START WITH UNCLEAR OBJECTIVES AND STRUCTURES

Enterprises spend billions on setting up and tracking progress with metrics. These efforts likely give those at the highest level at least some understanding of what's happening, but many of these metrics are too focused on the short term to be useful for those facing a complex, ambiguous challenge. Metrics are also chosen for their ability to be measured rather than for their appropriateness. Often the indicators we'd like to see for a collaboration aren't available to us. Matt LeMay, author of Agile for Everybody (O'Reilly), also points out that collaboration suffers from having "invisible ROI." He says that "trying to prove the contribution that healthy collaboration makes to an outcome is impossible, because we have no control group to compare it to. We don't know what would have happened if we hadn't worked together."

Rather than just following metrics, teams need clear objectives to steer their efforts. But creating clear objectives for an ambiguous problem isn't something many business people have mastered. It's natural, LeMay says, for people to offer up overly specific solutions as a starting point, but it can be a trap if the team doesn't know how to back up to the underlying vision that the effort is looking to achieve.

Collaboration can also be misunderstood as a freeform exchange of ideas, as embodied by the basic brainstorming meeting. Ideas are expected to be unleashed in a room full of people and the breakthrough made self-evident. In reality, open-ended brainstorms and free-ranging explorations are not very productive, and without any structure, people can fall into conflict, or conflict avoidance, very easily.

To help teams crack problems with unknown unknowns, we need to focus on framing the problem, stating objectives that describe outcomes (not outputs), and watching for leading indicators of longer-term success. Providing just enough structure and guardrails to help a team feel safe and have room to maneuver helps keep people focused.

EXPERTISE AND EXPERIENCE DOMINATE THE SOLUTION SPACE

Chi's guess-a-thon is the perfect example of how tempting it is to let experience and expertise rule the day. By giving over a decision to a specialist or expert, we may be helping ourselves avoid taking the blame if it turns out to be wrong. And then we hand it to a team to run with the expert's guess, which, because they know more than others, never gets revisited as the possible culprit when things fall apart.

Business has already acknowledged that things are more complex, as evidenced by its shift into more specialization and investments in technology. But it hasn't surrounded the specialists with the tools they need to get and share different perspectives. In most enterprises, the industrial age principles about division of labor and efficiencies are still in play. Leaders know what matters, and what success will look like when they see it. Workers fill in what's in between, never coloring outside the lines. Alan Cooper, author of *About Face* (Wiley), calls this "working forward" as opposed to backward, where leaders define what success looks like and leave the path for how to get there open to exploration and experimentation, not expertise. This open "whitespace" is key to getting teams to tackle complex problems and solve systemic issues that no single skill set can address.

One of the reasons we rely on experts is because we want to avoid conflict and criticism—both giving and receiving it. By deferring to the HIPPO (the highest-paid person's opinion) in the room, we let ourselves off the hook if there's a mistake.

But by giving in to experience and expertise, we miss an opportunity to share our work in early stages, making it accessible and understandable to others. It's the process of showing work in progress that helps us test our ideas and become aware of our assumptions. And when we begin to hear from others about how our work is being received, we start to get real data about our progress, instead of our wishful thinking.

Teams can better explore innovative solutions when they have the ability to open up constraints, have healthy discussions about solutions, and get real, actionable feedback on how well their solutions work.

INEFFECTIVE COMMUNICATION CAUSES CONFLICT

Building a common understanding among a potentially large and diverse group requires a great deal of communication. Many organizations know this, and have developed whole positions and systems to manage information across levels. But maintaining the flow of information can be time-consuming, and not very effective. I've noticed that as organizations scale, there's a tendency toward communicating status over outcomes because it's easier to manage and standardize.

A lot of communication also favors making decisions over transmitting knowledge. Josh Lovejoy ran efforts at both Amazon and Google to create standard design systems across very large teams. He points out that the typical approach to decision-making—where a series of short meetings focused on the highest priorities drive outcomes—doesn't help with decisions that are complex or nuanced. It means we choose the problems and solutions we can show progress on quickly. It means we bury those things we can't fit into our packed schedules until they inevitably erupt into crises.

Communication is also challenging when the participants aren't one size fits all. One of the biggest pitfalls I've seen is when teams are sharing with key stakeholders who haven't been intimately involved all along. Key stakeholders are often very powerful and influential, so teams seek their approval and endorsement without actually building any real understanding of the challenge and solution.

At the same time, some people aren't well suited to hashing questions out in a real-time, face-to-face situation. Different collaborators need different ways to explore ideas, provide feedback, and make decisions. The typical approach to gathering people around a table and holding a discussion may leave some perspectives unheard.

Leading collaborators communicate effectively by being transparent with those who are not deeply embedded in the effort so they stay aware enough to be useful and comfortable with what's happening.

How to Help Teams Avoid and Overcome Obstacles

As you'll learn throughout this book, there are steps you and your teams can take to avoid or overcome each of the obstacles just described (see Figure P-2). You can create or adapt your environment to be more inclusive and trusting, and use space in ways that promote better interactions. You can provide the right type of direction that teams need to manage their time, understand progress, and judge success. Help people be more creative and open to others' ideas so that your collaboration delivers on outcomes and doesn't just implement simple solutions that don't move the needle. And finally, you can improve the communication within the core group, and with key stakeholders, to reduce friction and keep people aligned.

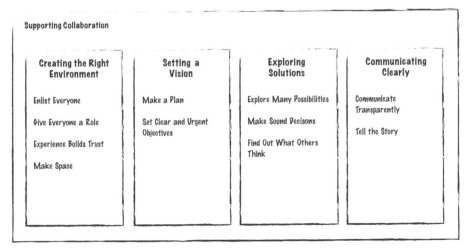

Figure P-2. Ways to support collaboration

PART I

Creating the Right Environment

The typical business setting, from the incentives it offers to its seating arrangements, is not naturally conducive to productive collaboration. The principles in this part will help you make the team feel safe and supported, and keep wider participation organized so that everyone can focus on the work at hand. The right environment means recruiting the right people, giving them a clear understanding of how they can contribute, building a sense of trust in the team, and using the (real and virtual) space you have wisely.

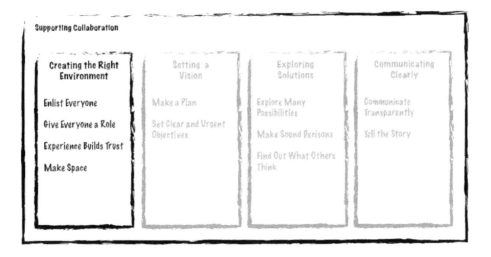

Enlist Everyone

This chapter will show how being more inclusive makes teams stronger by widening their perspective and making them more invested in the team's success. Managing groups of people who are very different can present some challenges and create conflict. You can take steps to help teams work through their differences, at least enough to make working together less painful, by enlisting everyone in a constructive way.

Now I know what you're thinking: *Everyone? That sounds...messy.* In meaningful collaborations "everyone" cannot literally mean *everyone*, but as a general principle the more you include people who are affected by, and invested in, the topic at hand, the better your results will be. Enlisting everyone, done right, actually helps.

Casting a wide net and including more people actually helps you move faster. That sounds counterintuitive, but consider for a moment that everyone may already be "helping" you, just not in a way that is *actually* helpful. Group dynamics, especially in competitive corporate culture, lead people to see efforts that exclude them as potential threats or a drain on resources that feel tight. At first, the people that you haven't engaged (for whatever reason) might stand off to the side, neither helping nor hurting your efforts. But it doesn't take much for those who feel excluded to stake out a position on the opposite bank, and work against what you are trying to do.

We tend to assume that anyone not working with us is a neutral party, but if those parties think they *should* be involved, they won't stay neutral. Often in a rush to just "get to it," we leapfrog over interested parties, only to find that we must spend large amounts of time and energy trying to get their buy-in later. Their participation takes place after the fact, in the form of combative reviews of "finished" work, or worse, competitive efforts that spring up and muddy the waters.

This isn't necessarily because these people don't believe in what you're doing. Rather, their reaction is a normal response to having a perspective that isn't being heard. When we have a real interest in an effort, we can't help but want to contribute, and if we aren't given a chance, it can bring up an emotional response that is hard to corral productively. By engaging "everyone" in approaching a problem, you increase their commitment to the end product and reduce the drag on momentum.

Including "everyone" doesn't mean every person is always fully involved, however: it means widening the funnel of inputs to the process, enlisting varied perspectives to generate solutions, and getting a larger set of people to vet ideas to find their faults and make your case stronger. Everyone *can* help if you make room for different perspectives and ways of engaging. Some people may be dedicating their full attention to the problem, pushing solutions forward, while others may be advising or providing feedback on work. The purpose of including everyone is to get a sufficiently diverse set of perspectives on a problem to mitigate risks and drive innovative solutions.

Enlist Everyone to Reduce Risks

A recent "innovation" from Doritos stands as a great reminder of how limiting the variety of orientations to a problem can have ridiculous results. The maker of tasty chips completed some customer research and found a surprising problem. Many women reported not feeling comfortable eating Doritos in public, saying that crunching loudly and licking the delicious chemical flavor powder from their fingertips just didn't seem ladylike. So the brand announced a plan to address this problem by creating Lady Doritos—a less crunchy, less finger-lickin' good version of the product. They had successfully dealt with every issue identified. Or had they?

Now, mind you, the problem wasn't that women weren't *buying* the chips, but that they had an aversion to eating them publicly. Both the analysis of the findings and the proposed solution stink of a team that lacks diversity. And I don't just mean women. I suspect that those involved were all "product people" whose only hammer is a new product type, and every nail a gap in the product line. Thankfully, the resulting internet backlash kept this idea from moving forward. Doritos could have avoided the PR gaffe, however, if they'd included people not responsible for product development in their team, because the issue is a messaging opportunity, not a product/market fit problem. A simple ad campaign showing women enthusiastically enjoying the chips in meetings, at the park, on the bus—all while smiling and laughing—would have gone a long way and probably required a lot less investment.

Blair Reeves, a Principal Product Manager at SAS and coauthor of *Building Products for the Enterprise: Product Management in Enterprise Software* (O'Reilly), says sometimes the blind spot comes in defining the very problem itself. Prior to getting into product management, Reeves worked in international development in Cameroon. He recalls how projects to improve infrastructure among communities often moved forward without partnership or input from the people within them. The so-called solutions may not have been used or sustained once implemented because the people didn't see them as something they had ownership of. When Reeves began asking communities about their priorities, he found that they were different than had been assumed. Issues like AIDS and HIV education weren't as big for them as his organization assumed; instead, the people wanted help with combating malaria and building latrines—issues that were more disruptive for them day-to-day.

Asking a diverse group that's closer to the problem is one way to spot and avoid potential missteps. A group that's too homogenous may make incorrect assumptions or apply too narrow a lens to finding solutions. You should also be sure that the team understands and seeks out the right skill sets, rather than assuming those skills are already present or blindly trying to "make do" with those that are.

Enlist Everyone to Boost Engagement

Including those who are affected by the outcomes of the work is also a boon to morale. Reeves not only discovered the community's real priorities, but also found that when he started asking people about the problem, they were easier to engage in the solutions. People we work with are no different. When you can invite more people to thoughtfully consider a problem or enlist their help to test solutions, they become more active and interested. It seems obvious that when people are shown or informed of work only once it's finished, they care less about it (unless, of course, they actively hate it), and yet sharing work that can't be changed much is standard for many office cultures.

Companies know that having more engaged employees is beneficial—that's why they spend so much time and money measuring engagement. Marc Benioff of Salesforce found his organization faced with the challenge (*http://bit.ly/2Xv7orv*) of employee engagement at senior levels of leadership, something that corporations pay a great deal of attention to. Higher engagement can multiply productivity and quality so much that substantial amounts of time and money are spent monitoring and supporting people's experience at work. Benioff wanted to nip his engagement problem in the bud, so he took pains to create a virtual space to understand what was fueling the issue and address it. He says, "In the end the dialogue lasted for weeks beyond the actual meeting. More important, by fostering a discussion across the entire organization, [I've] been able to better align the whole workforce around its mission. The event served as a catalyst for the creation of a more open and empowered culture at the company." Clearly, senior leaders at Salesforce are busy people whose typical focus is on the products and services they create, but without taking time to come together as a group and establish shared understanding and priorities, their day-to-day efforts would have been affected.

Collaboration is an approach to problem solving, but it's just as valuable as a cultural force that helps employees achieve purpose and meaning—not just productivity—in their jobs.

Enlisting Everyone Brings Up Cultural Differences

So, *maybe* enlisting "everyone" has some advantages, but employing this principle can also bring up issues around diversity and inclusion for the group. As a master of collaboration, it is important that you stay aware of dynamics that can reduce its benefits.

In the study of cultural differences, there's a force known as the *Power Distance Index*, first identified by business anthropologist Geert Hofstede, which measures the degree to which a group values hierarchy and ascribes power to leaders. A country like the US has relatively low power distance because we value flatter organization and independence over bowing to authority. Japan, on the other hand, rates very high, as the culture demands a great deal of respect for elders and authority.

In his book *Outliers* (Little, Brown and Company), Malcolm Gladwell tells the story of Korean Air's "cockpit culture" during the late 1990s, when the airline was experiencing more plane crashes than any other airline. Analysis showed that the cultural norm of giving in to superiors rather than challenging them meant that junior pilots who spotted problems failed to raise them. In *Fortune* (*http://bit.ly/2IIIfoJ*), Gladwell said:

What they were struggling with was a cultural legacy, that Korean culture is hierarchical. You are obliged to be deferential toward your elders and superiors in a way that would be unimaginable in the US.

But Boeing and Airbus design modern, complex airplanes to be flown by two equals. That works beautifully in low-power-distance cultures [like the US, where hierarchies aren't as relevant]. But in cultures that have high power distance, it's very difficult.

When the airline made some adjustments, their problem went away. They flattened out the Power Distance Index by reinforcing the value of junior aviators, and "a small miracle happened," Gladwell writes. "Korean Air turned itself around. Today, the airline is a member in good standing of the prestigious Sky-Team alliance. Its safety record since 1999 is spotless. In 2006, Korean Air was given the Phoenix Award by Air Transport World in recognition of its transformation. Aviation experts will tell you that Korean Air is now as safe as any airline in the world."

How we react to power isn't the only difference you're likely to run into. If you're beginning to see the value of widening the circle of collaborators and making sure they are active, respected participants, you might be wondering how to define the right level of "everyone" for your teams. Getting diversity means including people with a variety of:

- Experiences in industry and skills
- Cultural backgrounds
- Introversion and extroversion
- Working styles
- Primary languages
- Ownership, from end users to senior leaders and everyone in between

Helping teams deal with these differences requires being open to talking about differences, creating norms that bridge gaps, and having productive conflict. When people acknowledge to themselves and others where their perspective is coming from, it's easier for the group to not reject it as an outlier. Discussion about how the group will handle certain differences is also healthy. Creating explicit norms about everything from group versus individual working time to how decisions get made gives the group common ground. It's important to model, and hold each other accountable for, respecting these team norms.

Tools to Create the Right Environment for Collaboration: Tools to Help Enlist Everyone

Understanding what kind of team you have, how they think, and what they are missing is critical to being inclusive. Here are some tools you can use to set your team up and give them what they need to have a healthy, diverse environment.

Understanding Behavioral Differences: Variation 1

Knowing the skills that you have on the team and what you lack is key, but many times, the source of friction in teams is behavioral or cultural. It is useful to have the team identify and work through their issues with each other up front.

You will need small sticky notes, large sticky note pads or a whiteboard surface, and Sharpies for each person.

1. Ask each person to write down, one per sticky note, characteristics of the worst teams they have worked with.

2. Next, ask each person to write down aspects of the best, most high-performing team they have worked on.

3. Have each person present their negative and positive experiences to the team, grouping them together into negative and positive qualities on a large sticky note pad or under a heading on the whiteboard.

4. The facilitator should look for where people have alignment and divergence, grouping similar examples together to show the team where they agree and where they differ.

5. Review the items that are similar, and discuss what rule or norm the team would like to agree to. For example, if there's a lot of negativity around "too many meetings," establish specific times when meetings will be held, versus when people can have heads-down time.

6. Decide how to hold each other accountable for upholding the norms and what the consequences for breaking rules are. For example, is there a formal apology for missing meetings without prior notification?

7. Revisit the norms after a few weeks to see whether the team feels the need to change or add any new rules to help remove friction.

Understanding Behavioral Differences: Variation 2

If your team members aren't all comfortable sharing their experiences in prior teams (perhaps because some of them have worked together before, or are unwilling to speak up about negative feelings), consider this variation of the exercise to establish team norms.

In this exercise, you will have people identify their preferences or behaviors on several dimensions to see where there are similarities or differences. Then you can discuss and decide as a team what the shared expectation should be.

You will need small sticky notes, large sticky note pads or a whiteboard surface, and Sharpies for each person.

1. Create and label a horizontal line for each of the following categories, which are the main areas teams struggle over and typically develop norms around (see Figure 1-1):

    — **Interruptions.** How do team members feel about being interrupted with questions?

    — **Core Hours.** What are the hours the team should agree to be together in the office and/or available online? Team members may decide to work before or after core hours, as their schedules allow, but these are the hours that the team commits to each other.

    — **Meeting Times.** When should the team have typical meetings like stand-ups, weekly reviews, or other rituals?

    — **Authority and Decision-Making.** Who should make final decisions about important agreements for the team?

— **Disagreeing.** How comfortable are you with expressing disagreement about a decision?

— **Feedback.** How comfortable are you with receiving direct negative feedback?

2. Have each team member write their name or initials on a sticky note and place one (or in the case of indicating hours, two) on each line to indicate where their preferences fall.

3. Look at where there are overlaps and agreement, and where people diverge. Discuss these and create team norms accordingly.

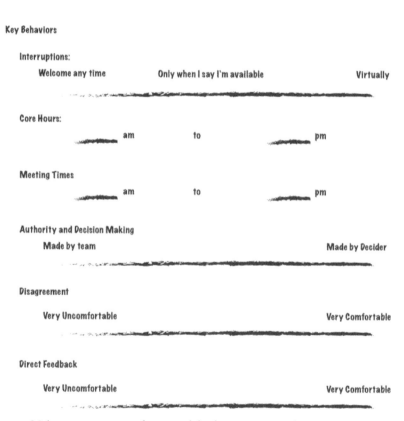

Figure 1-1. Main areas teams struggle over and develop norms around

Cross Cultures, Don't Overthrow Them

At some point in your journey to master collaboration, you will have a realization: people are a problem. Working with power structures can be challenging, especially if you don't happen to have a lot of authority in the system. And people are irrational and messy, which is why organizations create structures in the first place—to help guide our decisions and establish ways to control and command. Cyd Harrell, as someone who has made a big push in the last few years to bring innovation and inclusivity to the US government, knows all about these kinds of structures. As a leader at 18F, the digital services arm of the government, Harrell has worked with huge governmental agencies, elected officials, and political appointees, and she's seen firsthand the challenges of bringing a collaborative approach to command-and-control cultures.

"Some kinds of hierarchy are not conducive to good collaboration," she says, "but you have to find a way through anyway. That culture exists for a reason, and many of your stakeholders have a great deal invested in it." It's important to note that not all organizations are chasing less hierarchy and flatter structures. Civil servants and employees at government agencies typically have a much longer tenure than you find in Silicon Valley, and many people work hard for years to attain a level of authority and power—which they aren't eager to shove aside in the interest of being "transparent" and nonhierarchical. These organizations have succeeded in large-scale, often high-risk, situations because they employ what Harrell calls a "submit and review" approach, in which ideas are taken to a final state where a gatekeeper has the power to approve or reject them in a single blow. In that model, more senior people are seen as experts whose point of view demands organization-wide alignment. Conversely, those who are elected or appointed might serve short tenures with a great deal of authority, but priorities and perspectives change once that person has been replaced or voted out of office. Both of these forces tend to make collaboration hard, or nearly impossible.

But, Harrell says, at the same time, you can't get around these cultural forces. Approaching collaboration in this setting without respecting the system and structures is likely to have bad effects. When I offered some ideas I've seen used to break through power imbalances and help create a different vibe in a team, Harrell was quick to correct me. "You can't make changing the culture central to your success" in an environment where so many are so invested in its structure. And trying to get around it by going to a senior influencer might land you in hot water for violating the chain of command. Asking people lower on the totem pole to speak up in front of more senior people can also backfire, since the system doesn't reward new ideas as much as it rewards supporting the hierarchy.

The US government is one such culture, and during her tenure Harrell has learned how to navigate it rather than fight it. Her approach is simple: have a great deal of empathy for your stakeholders, however reluctant they are, and create a space where the normal rules and systems are paused or changed. Or, work within the command-and-control system, but constantly seek input and reviews from people along the way by asking for their expert input. The trick is to acknowledge to yourself and the team that the situation simply requires another iteration or two to bring the sticky stakeholder along. Since you are always showing "finished" work, you must be willing to be "wrong" so that you can have a meaningful conversation about what's not working and how it might be fixed.

But cultural differences can also be more geographically influenced, such as in teams that are large and international or dispersed. Erin Meyer is an author and researcher who's done a lot to map out the ways (*http://bit.ly/2tIWiAd*) in which cultures differ, which in turn helps us negotiate them. Her work is useful for those who are navigating national cultural differences in teams, from how to give negative feedback to how to build a schedule. More typically, though, teams are made up of people who differ culturally not only in terms of their countries of origin but also in their backgrounds and skills, so it may be most useful to focus on individual behaviors.

Some companies have collaboration built into their cultures from the start. Netflix began with an unusual business model—mailing customers DVDs of movies from their queue—and transitioned to streaming media at a time when physical media was losing adoption. The company has recently undergone another transition and begun creating their own movies and TV shows to stream. The resilience of their business model and technology are impressive, and much of the credit for the company's success is attributed to their strong culture, which values collaboration highly. This culture is embodied in a famous "deck" of slides that was shared openly on the internet and is now published on the company's website (*https://jobs.netflix.com/culture*). Andrea Mangini, Director of Product Design, offered her observations about how that culture works on the inside, as someone relatively new to the company. She says that people are constantly showing their work and inviting others to weigh in. People value getting feedback; in fact, not seeking out the opinions of others is frowned upon. Because the emphasis on collaboration has been at the core of the company since the start, it's second nature to many employees. The company sees so much value in breaking down silos that they're not as concerned about duplicating efforts and optimizing the creation of new ideas.

No matter your environment, by being intentional about involving "everyone" and making your differences productive through team norms, you get the diversity you need while maintaining the sanity you deserve. By understanding power differences and openly discussing cultural differences—whether they are based on nationality, background, or skill set—you will help create a more harmonious collaboration.

Troubleshooting Issues with Enlisting Everyone

Bringing many different people together can surface many emotional and interpersonal issues in the team and with stakeholders. This section discusses some ideas you can use to mitigate these issues and keep the team focused.

DEALING WITH DIFFICULT PEOPLE IN TEAMS

However you've decided to set up your core team, it's likely that at some point, one or more members will turn out to be trouble. Whether it's someone who dominates or someone you can't seem to get to speak up, difficult people are a fact of collaborative life. Thorsten Borek and his team at Neon Sprints in Hamburg, Germany, have created a simple framework to understand the problematic people who show up to collaborate (or not, as we'll see). I have recreated their framework here with permission because it's simply too useful not to share. The framework has five main types of difficult people, and ways you can handle them gracefully:

The leader
> Leaders can't help but take over in a meeting, controlling conversations and dominating ideas. Whether they are literally the boss or just act like it, their presence is likely stifling to others and a pain to facilitate. The key here is to understand that their motivations are *power-driven*, meaning that they seek to be seen as powerful by others. To handle leaders, Borek suggests giving them an important task—the keyword being *important*. These folks should be asked to lead a discussion about key decision criteria, or to make critical decisions.

The know-it-all
> Know-it-alls are those who constantly drag the discussion in a specific direction or bring up what seems like minutia when the group is talking

about the big picture. They make other participants cringe because they take things off-track even though they may be saying important things. Understand that these people are *knowledge-driven*, and need a way to channel and share their expertise with the group productively. Handling know-it-alls means giving them an outlet in a collaboration. Consider giving them a chance to present their knowledge of constraints as part of framing a problem, or let them share insights about a specific technology you are considering. Truly disruptive people may need to be handled with care, and included only in places where they won't drown everyone else out all the time.

The introvert

You may not always notice introverts as problems in your team, because they tend to be nice and quiet, eagerly following along and agreeing with whatever the last person said. Introverts are *instruction-driven*, meaning they may not be extroverted or confident enough to participate in messy, free-form discussions. Giving them very clear instructions, or running through an exercise together before asking them to do it on their own, will help build up their comfort level and confidence. They can also be enlisted to help out the group in many ways, since they highly value helping the group get along.

The negativist

Negativists are people who, no matter what, can't help but resist what is happening every step of the way. These people will question the process being used ad nauseum, or insist that every idea offered has already been tried. Often these folks are *resistance-driven* because they've not been listened to, either by you or by others in the past. Handle negative people with care, making them into valued experts and enlisting them to prepare and strategize ahead of time. But these people may also prove difficult to change, so consider asking them to serve as a critic of the effort, rather than an idea generator, to best take advantage of their energy.

The indecisive

This type of team member typically is well integrated in how the team works and eager to participate in discussions. Frequently indecisives will introduce different perspectives on a subject or ask to consider more aspects of the matter at hand. However, when asked to make a decision, they have a really hard time making up their mind. And once they do decide, in 9 out of 10 cases they'll ask to change that decision after a few minutes, potentially asking the team for more input "just to be sure." The indecisive team member is *safety-driven* and needs constant reassurance about proceedings and decisions.

It's worth getting to know your team members and stakeholders well enough to understand what they value and what drives them. You can do this in a variety of ways—from 1:1 interviews, to asking people who have experience with individuals what they think, to trying out different approaches and seeing what works.

HANDLING A CRITICAL STAKEHOLDER WHO WON'T ENGAGE

Sometimes, despite your invitations, a person just won't show interest or participate in the effort. Many people I spoke to described having an important stakeholder or subject-matter expert either fail to attend sessions (even short ones) or express deep skepticism of the enterprise.

The cause of this lack of engagement can vary. Often it's just that these stakeholders have competing priorities, and yours doesn't rise to the top of the pile. This happens with people whose expertise is in high demand. When I dug in with one such person, I learned that their days had a *Groundhog Day* quality, where they were called upon over and over again to deliver the same perspective, the same information across many groups, and each new request felt even less interesting and valuable than the last.

So what can I do?

Understand their priorities
> When you can't get the attention of someone critical to the effort, it's worth spending some time trying to understand what they are devoting attention to. You can frame your project in ways to align with what they care about to get more support. You can do this by speaking with them directly, but if they aren't engaging with you, try speaking to those around them who are likely to know what their focus is. It also may be necessary to acknowledge that their other priorities are more important. You may need to wait until they have the time and space to devote to your effort.

Burn a cycle
> When a key stakeholder won't give you the time of day because they don't believe the work is needed, trying to force them to play ball probably won't work. Instead, run through a cycle of exploration to move quickly from the

fuzzy frontend questions and assumptions to asserting a hypothesis about the solution or creating a prototype. This answer need not be (and probably won't be) the right one, so beware of investing a lot of time or making it very high-fidelity. What you might find is that once you assert a "truth" developed by the collaboration, you'll suddenly get the stakeholder's attention—although it's likely to be negative. But this is the time to make sure that person feels like their input and knowledge is what's required to solve the problem. When I work with people in complex domains, I often show them things early on that are wrong or incomplete so that they'll be compelled to step in to provide guidance and fill in what's missing. If you prepare yourself to take an extra cycle or two to draw people in, you save yourself the frustration of having more finished work "rejected" by someone who could have been helpful earlier on.

Join forces or have a runoff

As a consultant, I've been hired by large organizations a shocking number of times to work on problems that other people were already trying to solve. When you discover this, consider merging or aligning your efforts with the other team(s) in the spirit of sharing the load to move faster. Or, alert leadership about the redundancy, because it may be something they aren't aware of. In my experience, however, this isn't always a case of the right hand not knowing what the left hand is doing. Some companies intentionally set up different teams to see what different solutions emerge. In this case, you should know your work is in a runoff, and proceed anyway. Make sure that the ideas are being compared fairly, though—try to ensure that leaders aren't comparing the cookie dough from one team with the freshly baked cookies from another. It also may be a good idea to reach out to the other teams so everyone understands what's happening.

MANAGING SOMEONE WHO IS SPREAD TOO THIN

Having team members who are spread too thin will stress any team. One of the strengths of Agile/Sprint methodology is the insistence on 100% dedication to the team. This is a great goal, but all too often I run into people who have too much on their plates. When your collaborators have varying levels of dedication to the cause, you may run into resentment ("X isn't pulling their weight") or dismay ("I want to do more, but I can't!").

So what can I do?

Speak to a manager

You can try to ask the person who oversees the employee to help clear the person's plate, for everyone's sanity. Don't do this behind the employee's back, but rather include them in the discussion about how everyone wants to make sure priorities are aligned. This isn't the employee's problem, it's the resource manager's.

Spread the gospel for them

When a key player is trapped in a cycle of being the subject-matter expert, you can help them by aggregating some of their requests for them, and aligning their input sessions (at least up front) into a single learning session so they can get off the hamster wheel. You could also offer to attend meetings with other groups to consolidate. And, while you're there, consider recording video and compiling great notes that they can use as a first line of defense for requests for their time. This should also serve to create a bond, and hopefully they'll repay you by giving you just enough attention later.

Change their status

If someone really can't be spared the needed time to focus on your collaboration, then it's a good idea to be explicit about making them an advisor who can review and weigh in, but who isn't part of the core team. It's also worth seeing if they have a protégé or colleague who might be better able to participate, even if that person's at a lower level of expertise.

NAVIGATING CULTURAL CONFLICTS

The main objective of many personnel managers is to minimize dust-ups between employees and promote healthy teams—the irony being, of course, that avoiding conflict ends up creating more issues than it solves. If the business of business were really without contention, and everyone agreed all the time, then we could have delegated it all to robots and retired in our utopia long ago. But the reality is, we need to express and work through differences of opinion to get to better answers—the very heart of what this book is about.

But what happens when your teams, whether intrinsically or through coaching, won't fully engage in healthy debate? If you notice that there are few points of disagreement in your team, it's time to stir the pot. Otherwise, productivity will actually suffer, as energy spent *not* arguing takes away from accomplishing goals.

You need to strike a balance among team members where there is productive tension and conflict about specific ideas, not individual people.

So what can I do?

Talk cross-culturally

A lot of what underlies the willingness to speak up, or not, may be cultural. In the spirit of openness, it might be a good idea for your team to spend time together talking openly about what their expectations are, and sharing their previous experiences. Erin Meyer has fantastic advice in her book, *The Culture Map* (PublicAffairs), and online (*http://bit.ly/2EuKVB1*) about helping teams embrace productive conflict despite cultural differences. She suggests using specific language, like "Help me understand your point" in place of "I disagree with that," to depersonalize and invite intellectual discussion among those who might otherwise give in.

Map it out

Meyer also suggests mapping out the differences in the team explicitly. Her model is specific to national cultural differences, which may be both irrelevant and overly simplistic for your purposes. But if you replace the nationalities with specific team members and their individual predispositions, you can use this tool to help team members better understand where they're each coming from.

Remove the boss

Some people may be more reticent to express themselves when an authority figure is in the room. Help your diverse teams feel comfortable by making sure they have space to engage with each other where they don't feel like they are being watched or need to align with a superior.

Establish team norms

Establishing team norms about things like when meetings will be held, or what the definition of "done" is, is a key practice. For managing conflict, it can be good to discuss and decide what the team considers healthy, and not, when facing a conflict. I've seen norms such as "Ask for explanations over offering attacks" that are the result of a diverse team striving to be inclusive of different views.

Work asynchronously.
Some conflict arises when people try to do too much all together. Keep an eye on people's energy levels, be aware of those who may do better work on their own, and then come back to share and critique. Make time and space for people to be away from one another and keep their discussion focused on the content of work and decisions.

Conclusion

Collaboration at its core is about including diverse perspectives and people. Being inclusive makes teams stronger; you have more to draw on and get more people invested in the success of the effort. But groups often need help bringing their differences together productively. You can help teams be open with each other and develop shared norms to govern behaviors. You can also model what respecting differences and healthy tension looks like so that the group doesn't just stick to what's "safe" because it's easier. In the next chapter, we'll look at how to give people clear roles to channel their energies and contribute to a healthier environment.

Key Takeaways

- Being inclusive of many different kinds of people, skill sets, and perspectives is a core part of collaboration that helps mitigate risks, engage the team, and find blind spots before they become a problem.

- Inclusivity can challenge the status quo of how people interact and may bring about interpersonal conflicts that are destructive to the team.

- Working in different cultures that aren't naturally conducive to collaboration is challenging, but don't get caught up in making changing the culture your mission. Instead, focus on practical, tactical changes that create a local space for teams to be productive and deliver results. Culture change will happen as a by-product of good results over time.

2

Give Everyone a Role

In the last chapter, we looked at how encouraging diversity in a team helps generate and test ideas more easily and quickly, but can bring up conflict in some cases. Establishing clear roles for people helps channel their energies and can reduce unproductive tension around different responsibilities. In this chapter you'll learn how to approach assembling different collaborators, and how to use explicit roles to channel different skills and impulses.

Christina Wodtke, founder of Balanced Team, points out that "we know how to channel people from a skill set perspective—designers design and developers write code. But, if nonfunctional roles aren't delineated, there's guaranteed to be conflict." She says clear roles deal with things like, "Who makes decisions? Who brings what perspectives? Who's able to facilitate openly? Who will plan and track what the collaborators do?" Wodtke also acknowledges that roles are never a set piece that can work anywhere. "Different collaborations will have different shapes," she says, calling up classic comic book collaborations as an example. Stan Lee and Steve Ditko, pioneers of comic book creation, approached writing and drawing together as two equals with different skills building one thing. Sci-fi and fantasy author Neil Gaiman, on the other hand, will turn over a full manuscript for a graphic novel without really having thought much about what the visuals should or would be. Both approaches clearly result in quality output, but each is suited to the individual collaborators.

There are some conventional role definition frameworks that can be used/adapted for collaboration success, as well as some roles that don't typically get called out in such frameworks but are critical nonetheless. At the end of the day, roles formally establish authority and scope in a way that the whole team can share. The importance of roles lies in their ability not only to channel power dynamics, but also to create growth opportunities for more junior team members or people looking to expand their skills.

Next we'll look at how roles help channel people's energy and clarify boundaries and responsibilities within the team to keep everyone focused and productive. Roles should be defined both for those who are fully focused on the effort as well as for stakeholders and experts that advise the team. Roles aren't like job functions that are stable; over time, you may find that they can shift to give people different experiences.

Levels of Contribution

When you are enlisting everyone, as we looked at in Chapter 1, there is a time and place for many people to participate, but there are also times when it's more appropriate for a smaller, core group of people to dive into solutions. It pays to be clear about different levels of contribution, as shown in Figure 2-1.

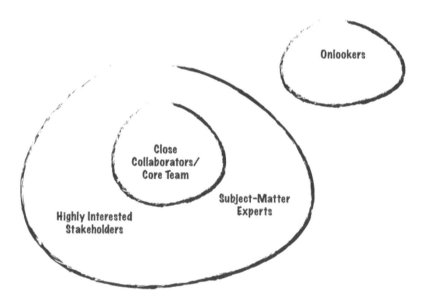

Figure 2-1. A model for understanding different types of collaborators

At the center of this model, you have the inner circle of *close collaborators*, who do the bulk of the heavy lifting. This is where a few people who are very close to the problem explore ideas and develop them to be tested. These are the people who are focused on the problem fully, and who have the diverse skills needed to create solutions for it. The roles here need to support a balance between exploring divergent ideas and converging and testing ideas in a way that is traceable and transparent.

Surrounding the close collaborators are *highly interested stakeholders*, who are collaborators in the effort even if they aren't directly responsible for delivering the solution. In other words, these people are affected by the outcome of the collaboration but aren't actively participating on a daily basis. They might be people who manage a critical function or effort that has dependencies or related priorities. The biggest challenge that arises here is when these stakeholders are not clear on how they are to participate, especially senior leaders who are accustomed to having their casual remarks about ideas or solutions taken as clear directives. Establishing the lines of authority around decisions and feedback mechanisms is critical.

On the outside are *onlookers* who are watching your collaboration even if they haven't been invited to participate. This may be because they are inspired by the effort, fearful of being left out, or simply bored and looking for a distraction. While it can be tempting to ignore these folks, it's useful to make sure you are communicating to this audience so they don't become active detractors.

It's important to point out that collaborators aren't necessarily those within your direct organization. You'll likely have to include clients, or outside partners with specific expertise. There isn't necessarily a big difference in how people work together from different companies, but it is worth noting that their goals may be generally aligned but still not 100% the same as yours. For example, a vendor you rely on for key technology needs a seat at the table, but success for them may be selling you more product versus your end product being successful.

The next sections go into more detail about assigning roles for those who work closely together on the problem "full time," versus those stakeholders, subject-matter experts, and onlookers who need a different structure to guide their less frequent participation.

Roles for Close Collaborators

From Agile to sprints to design thinking, there's a great deal out there about how to get close collaborators working well together. I have found that, when it comes to making use of roles, the world of *pairing* has a lot of value. *Pair programming* is a movement that started with software developers as a way to increase the quality of code and to move quickly through a variety of approaches to a problem. *Pair design* takes a similar approach to the architecture and overall design of a product or service. Pairing can be practiced by designers, developers, and product managers. In our book *Pair Design* (*https://www.oreilly.com/ideas/pair-design*), Chris Noessel and I look at how pairing works and show some variations of how it is practiced in detail. For our purposes, it's less about people working in literal pairs than giving small groups of two to five collaborators structure for their participation in an intimate team. The roles described next can help your team share responsibilities for working together as a core team. These roles aren't about specific skills, but rather serve as a way to focus different people working in a small group.

THE NAVIGATOR

Every journey needs a navigator, whether you're heading out on a well-mapped road trip or charting unknown territory. And yet, most of the time, we think more about the driver who's getting us from A to B than the person making sure we actually arrive in the right place. In small groups of close collaborators, you should have one person designated as the navigator.

This role can be expansive or focused, depending on the context. At its most minimal, it involves tracking decisions and rationale and the process of how the group works. Like a lab book for a science course, it helps you make sure you have enough of a record to back up any findings you might discover. Navigators should focus on:

- Keeping track of the overall strategic direction of the work
- Documenting key decisions and rationale
- Communicating solutions, progress, understanding of context, and the problem the team is solving for
- Telling the story about how the work has progressed, what struggles were overcome, and what's changed as a result

When you're assigning the role of navigator, there are several traits you should look for and actively support. This role carries a great deal of responsibility for keeping the whole together and being a credible source of documenting and presenting ideas. It can be a good role for more junior people who show promise and are looking for new responsibilities. Obviously in situations where communicating the collaboration is large-scale and critical, you should bring in people with more experience. Navigators should be:

Detail-oriented

Navigators must be detail-oriented and take seriously the job of keeping information for the group.

Organized

Navigators must be able to track (or even, in some cases, create) the course and progress of the work in order to loop in those outside the circle enough that they don't try to undermine or solely nitpick it.

Strong communicators

The navigator is the natural person to be the "emcee" of the group, setting context in presentations so that other members can deliver more details about solutions.

You can help those playing the role by making sure they have a supportive environment:

Dedicated time

Make sure they have the time and focus to track information.

Real-time, transparent capture

Encourage real-time capture and prompt synthesis. Navigators should function as the team historian, pulling together enough of what's happened to build a story about how the team got there, not just where they arrived.

Focus

Help navigators focus on recording the *right* stuff, not *all* the stuff.

THE DRIVER(S)

If the navigator within a collaboration is focusing on the bigger picture for the group to explore, the driver is the person (or people) working through possible solutions to the challenges within that space. There should be only one navigator, but there may be multiple drivers generating ideas. They will be holding the pen at the whiteboard, or using the keyboard to write code or draw ideas quickly. Drivers are less concerned with tracking the flow or keeping the whole picture in mind than navigators, focusing instead on developing divergent approaches to a problem quickly so that the group can evaluate them.

Drivers are typically responsible for:

Technical solutions
Developing ideas and creating them (in code, on whiteboard, etc.).

Expansive thinking
Developing multiple approaches to a solution rather than simply homing in on one. This is where having several drivers is useful.

Bringing expertise.
Having more specific perspectives on the problem and solution space.

When assigning the driver role, you are looking for people who have enough technical ability to render their ideas quickly in some medium for the pair or small group to react to. Drivers should also be able to easily come up with multiple solutions to a challenge, not zero in on a single idea and argue it. Drivers should be:

Fluent in the medium
Whether you are developing a new organizational model or creating a new feature for a product, drivers should have the requisite technical skills and knowledge to create substantive artifacts.

Solution-focused
Whether your driver(s) are extroverts who enjoy duking it out over ideas at the whiteboard, or more internal processors who need to work "offline" to generate ideas to critique, their job is to give options, not rehash assumptions or redraw the map.

Invested in group success
Driving is not about winning. Drivers should not be made to think they're leading the team or competing to come up with *the* solution.

Free to work in the style that suits them best
Note that not all drivers need to be highly verbal types who think on their feet. Drivers who are more introverted may need to develop ideas on their own and then bring them back to the group to share and critique.

It's worth noting that, at least during early stages, this circle of close collaborators may be three or four (or even five!) people. When there's more than a handful of people who have a great deal of trust and respect, it's more likely that you're workshopping ideas with a group that involves some stakeholders than actually doing deep, close collaboration. In these cases, you should be very clear about who the navigator is, and assign all others to be drivers. In a group of three or four, you might try having people work "alone, together" as Jake Knapp calls it in his book *Sprint* (PCC). In this vein, rather than having a pair work tightly out loud on the problem, you would have people work for a bit on developing ideas and sharing them, have a critique led by the navigator, and then refine the ideas iteratively in the group. It is a good idea to state clearly that all drivers in that setting are equals, even if there are technically more senior and more junior people in the role. As the master of collaboration, you can help the driver or drivers succeed by:

Killing egos

Model what it looks like to focus on group success; use group retrospectives to keep big egos in check and help others feel heard.

Together time/alone time

Most successful pairings I've seen have a schedule that might have people work closely together for a few hours in the morning, and then have them work independently in the afternoon. When they return the next day, they can check in about where each partner got to.

Dedicated focus

Like navigators, drivers need enough time and space to take the ideas that the pair has worked through to the next level. If drivers are spread across multiple problems, you'll find that they resort to "swoop and poop" behavior (see Chapter 7) rather than being invested in the specific problem and pair.

Finally, when wrangling people in very close collaboration, be aware that these roles can (and in some cases, should) be fluid. Especially later in the process when the collaboration is about specific implementations of solutions as opposed to a big vision, it can be useful to have people take different perspectives and switch often. Sometimes this happens naturally. When observing pair programming, I've seen two people working the same keyboard and mouse because each person is very familiar with the problem and has skills or expertise specific to solving it. There are also pairs who fit so naturally into the roles that no swapping happens. Often if one of the collaborators is a product manager or has another generalist skill set, they will fit naturally into the role of navigator and won't have the technical expertise or fluency to be a driver. If you are filling one of the roles of close collaboration, make sure you yourself are keeping to your assigned role, and check in often to make sure you haven't lost sight of the path you are navigating.

CRITICS

We've all had the colleague who just can't help but shut down every idea that they encounter. Whether it's because "we already tried that" or "it's not possible," they've never met a solution they like. Their energy isn't just annoying, it can infect the entire group by making people doubt themselves or exhaust themselves having to debate endlessly with someone who won't engage.

Explicitly assigning someone the critic role can turn their negativity into something productive, but it takes some doing. You must first decide when to assign this role. If you know that someone it's important to include is likely to be a naysayer, approach them ahead of time and tell them you specifically want them to take this position. Be sure to frame it as a critical part of the process, explaining that you want to harness their expertise to find weaknesses in the solution set so it can be refined.

If the resistance appears during the process of defining the objective or generating divergent options, you will have to try to reframe their participation after the fact, which can be awkward. I find it helpful to explain the overall process and timeframe of the effort, and be clear about when they will be called upon. You can give them a specific meeting or series with the group for them to "lead" their critiques. It's important to remove them from the meetings where that energy won't be welcome. I tend to say something like, "You can skip tomorrow's session. We're going to be doing more brainstorming, which is going to drive you crazy. Feel free to leave this part of the process to us, and we'll share what we come up with afterward. We'd love to hear your thoughts in next week's session."

The trick is elevating their negative energy into an official part of the process. Help critics feel valued and be useful by:

Being rigorous

Give them specific guidance on how to frame their feedback. List out specific questions you are looking for them to answer about the work so they know where to focus. It also helps to be clear about where in the process the work is, and what assumptions you've made along the way.

Letting them air their reservations

Don't give in to the tendency to argue with their critique. The points that are valid can be used to make solutions stronger. Points that are conjecture or strawman arguments can be ignored.

Giving them dedicated space

Ask critics to lead a specific session to tackle ideas, versus interrupting while the team is generating options. It can also be useful to ask them to write down their arguments, or comment on what others have written rather than do it all face to face.

Testing their theories

Remember that in general, the critic's arguments are just as much a guess as the ideas they critique. Enlist the critic to help test ideas out and identify what evidence is needed to categorize an idea as good, bad, or impossible.

Celebrating their improvements

When a critique does make ideas better, be sure to call that out. That is something the whole team should feel good about.

THE FACILITATOR

In addition to a navigator, you may need a separate facilitator to guide discussions—most often when the core group of close collaborators are bringing in stakeholders or subject-matter experts to explore ideas and give feedback. Most facilitation experts see the key responsibility of this role as guiding the process, with less focus on the content of the problem area or solution. Appoint a facilitator to wrangle larger groups, especially if there are many different levels of seniority, authority, and expertise coming together. If you or those you work with will not be seen as impartial, and the challenge is highly charged or political, consider hiring a facilitator or finding someone in the org who is seen as impartial and can be a trusted facilitator.

Facilitators are primarily responsible for:

- Structuring and managing time
- Keeping focus on the material and appropriate topics
- Keeping discussions and decisions visible (working with navigator)
- Helping the group make "lasting agreements" and move through the diverge/converge process together

When choosing a facilitator, look for someone who can stay above the fray and keep the big picture in mind. You, as someone who is curious about successful collaboration, are a likely candidate for this role. Facilitators tend to be:

Above the fray
> A facilitator is a guide to help people move through a process together, not the seat of wisdom and knowledge. That means a facilitator isn't there to give opinions, but to draw out opinions and ideas from the group members.

Invested in the team
> Facilitators focus on how people participate in the process of learning or planning, not just on what gets achieved.

Open-minded
> A facilitator is neutral and never takes sides.

If you feel like you aren't this person, or maybe don't feel like you have enough political clout to pull it off, the navigator is another role to consider where you can hone your leadership skills.

RACI Models for Stakeholders and Supporters

Many organizations use a model known as RACI to organize their decision-making. To summarize it briefly, RACI is an acronym that encapsulates each of these key roles:

Responsible
> The person who fully understands the challenge and desired outcome, and who is accountable for the success of the effort. Without adequate incentive to make "winning" decisions or be accountable, this person serves more of

a facilitative role. As the person who arguably is closest to the problem and the possibilities, they benefit from having the risk/reward of making the right decisions, or more likely, learning from decisions to get to the right decision.

Accountable (or the advisor)

The person (or people) who are positioned to understand the risk implications of different decisions, who have veto authority, and who are aware of how outcomes affect the company. I have found that while the CEO might be ultimately accountable for a decision, assigning them the explicit accountability role means they rarely have enough information to question the ideas of the driver. To this end, making them instead an advisor who can veto or challenge ideas sets them up as a contractive foil to the driver, and makes them less likely to blindly accept their recommendations or argue for argument's sake.

Consulted (or contributors)

These are people who are responsible for actually developing solutions to challenges and seeing them implemented. They will certainly include the close collaborators we looked at previously. This category may also include those who are responsible for aspects of the solution that are dependent on, or highly related but adjacent to, the core solution (such as platform engineering or members of the legal team). Often contributors are actually those who inhabit the creation-oriented roles described earlier, such as drivers or navigators or critics.

Informed

This group tends to be overlooked and dismissed in the (mistaken) assumption that they are less important that the others. However, as we will see, and you likely have experienced, if those who should be informed don't feel adequately prepared, they are likely to become bottlenecks or adversaries who need to be won over after the fact.

Note

You may have seen or read about this model as DACI instead of RACI. In a DACI model, the *R* becomes a *D*, for the decider or driver of the effort. Given the previous discussion of pairing or close collaboration, I use RACI's "Responsible" category to avoid confusion about this role. In my experience, and in the experience of those I spoke with, the differences are negligible between the two sets of acronyms. The key is to assign different focuses to those who have a great deal of accountability for a solution, but little hands-on time or experience, and those who work on a problem directly. Having seen this model employed in many different settings, I have seen it provide healthy clarity around decisions and help teams work in smaller groups, with less friction with those who are *interested* and perhaps want to be more than *informed*.

Things to consider when assigning roles and putting the group together:

Expertise and skills
> You need a variety but also need to cover what's required to get the job done. Even if you can't get full participation from someone with critical knowledge or abilities, see what time and attention you can get rather than trying to make do.

Ability to think on their feet versus "offline" and on their own
> If the entire group loves to debate verbally and intensely, you may find that ideas are being chosen based on that public performance, without careful analysis. See who might be able to work offline or in writing to bring a different lens.

Language proficiency
> If not everyone shares the same native language, see if you can get the group to use simple words and syntax, avoiding acronyms or abbreviations that won't be well known.

By being thoughtful about how you place people in a team, and being prepared ahead of time, you can channel people's energy more productively.

Troubleshooting Roles

Assigning roles and getting people to stay in them is key to keeping people aligned and coordinated. This section describes ideas for how to handle issues within the core team and with stakeholders.

ASSUMED HIERARCHY IN THE TEAM

While there's nothing inherent in any of the roles I've described that specifically calls out one as more important than another, people may still think that way. Because our corporate culture tends to celebrate individuals who lead by speaking frequently and making decisions, it's natural to assume a hierarchy that doesn't need to be there. After all, no one can make a well-informed decision about something complex without the contributors who put in blood, sweat, and tears to lay out the options. While according to the org chart there may be an actual hierarchy in a group, the point of roles is often to establish different, more inclusive lines of authority that make room for those "at the bottom." When people start assuming that some roles are more important than others in a collaboration, it's not just a morale killer, it's a perspective killer.

So what can I do?

Rotate roles

One way to make it clear that all roles are valued—as are all people in a team—is to have people swap roles from time to time. This is less applicable to the RACI roles, which should remain stable among a group of people who aren't working on an issue day-to-day. But asking navigators to be drivers for a cycle can help people see the value of both roles. It's also a good way to give people experience doing things they may not naturally be drawn to or excel at. Asking someone who's used to only generating ideas to instead serve as the "big picture" person for a while may give them some empathy for how hard that role can be. Likewise, those who don't think of themselves as creative may be surprised at their ability to open up when they're freed from charting the team's path. This can be especially useful if there is a group of three or four people who are co-creating something and there is a natural set of alliances that emerge. "Forcing" people to shift their role will also help them shift their perspective and perhaps be able to get beyond their default position to achieve a breakthrough. Rotating roles also helps people skill up and grow their capabilities.

Model and celebrate being a "contributor"

When RACI roles are assigned, there's often much more attention paid to who gets to decide things, and who gets to advise on or veto them. You can help draw energy away from these roles by calling out key contributions that the team needs, whether it's expertise or key deliverables. When you yourself are a contributor, take great pride in knowing that the "real work" you are doing moves the needle as much as any leader's input. Good senior leaders are very willing to share the limelight and call out the efforts of contributors, especially if you ask them to.

ROLES GET IGNORED

Just because you've assigned roles doesn't mean they're always respected. Especially over time, people can fall into natural ruts and let roles fall by the wayside. Or, people take on responsibilities that rightfully belong to others because they are easier or seen to be more prestigious.

So what can I do?

Look for a mismatch
> You may have a person who's been put in a role that's a bit of a stretch for them. Perhaps that was an intentional move to give them a growth opportunity, or perhaps they overcommitted themselves. It may be worth revisiting roles and adjusting responsibilities temporarily or for the longer term.

Commit to responsibilities as a group
> If it feels like the person or people aren't "staying in their lane" out of laziness or willful ignorance, have the group periodically review different roles and commit to them explicitly. When people have to sign up for something publicly, that gives the group the ability to hold them accountable, or gives them the needed prod to hold *themselves* accountable.

Conclusion

Roles help channel people's energy and clarify boundaries and responsibilities, so it's worth taking the time to define them and make sure they are understood. Having a set of roles for close collaborators will help them work through defining problems and generating ideas. For stakeholders and other interested parties, RACI roles provide structure to discuss and make decisions productively. It's important to note that roles aren't positions, and can and should flex over time, giving people different experiences and areas of focus. In the next chapter we'll look at how to help teams develop trust in each other so they can persevere when things get tough or uncomfortable.

Key Takeaways

- Collaborations include differing levels of contribution. Not everyone is focused on the problem full-time, so it's good to distinguish between the core team of close collaborators and the stakeholders and subject-matter experts that support them.

- Close collaborators need roles that keep them focused on their contributions when defining objectives and exploring ideas.

  — The navigator role holds down the big picture and directs the team's efforts to explore ideas and generate solutions to be tested.

  — The driver(s) role focuses people on the solutions to the problem and thinking creatively.

  — The historian role keeps track of what the team has done, and what it has discovered, to help tell the story later.

  — Critics are those who help evaluate ideas and bring in constraints to make them stronger.

  — The facilitator role focuses on the process and team dynamics, rather than the content of the collaboration, to keep things flowing and keep conflicts productive.

- For stakeholders and subject-matter experts who might be tempted to be overly prescriptive and dictate solutions, the RACI model helps with making decisions, establishing accountability, and knowing who should be informed along the way.

3

Enable Trust and Respect

This chapter looks at how trust helps teams come through adversity, and be more open to sharing ideas and getting to a breakthrough. Trust isn't something you can inject into people, but there are things you can do to help seed and support its growth. Learning how to lead teams in ways that enable trust, instead of diminishing it, is critical to collaboration. Working closely with people who are quite different from you can feel uncomfortable, but being able to work through differences yields great results; it just takes a little time and experience together to get there.

No one knows this better than Jimmy Chin, a photographer and filmmaker who is known for his work with athletes in extreme situations. His first major film, *Meru*, tells the story of three alpinists on their first ascent of an especially challenging peak in the Himalayas. The endeavor was so tough that they faced death multiple times before succeeding. His second film, the Oscar-winning *Free Solo*, captures a premier rock climber, Alex Honnold, climbing the 3,000-foot-high sheer rock face of Yosemite's El Capitan—without ropes or protection of any kind. What stands out in these extremely risky endeavors is the deep trust between the teammates, because they are quite literally putting their lives in each other's hands.

But Chin's collaborations aren't limited to the rock faces he shoots on. He produces his films with his wife, Elizabeth Chai Vasarhelyi, an award-winning documentary filmmaker herself with seven titles under her belt, including *Incorruptible*, which follows the youth resistance movement in Senegal in 2015. When Chin was developing *Meru*, his wife saw that while the raw footage of the incredible story was compelling, the film needed a narrative arc and emotional connection to bring it to life, so she stepped in to deliver that. The pair now works more formally together, with Chin handling the shoots on location and Vasarhelyi driving the editing and story creation, as Chin explains:

> On **Free Solo**, I needed to be the one to put together the crew to film Alex's climb. It took everything I've learned in last 20 years to put together. I needed to know what it feels like to be on both sides of the camera and how it affects your climbing. Chai's got deep experience in the nonfiction documentary space; she gets the emotional narrative and structure of the story and has objectivity about the climbing aspects. She's extraordinary at that craft and I trust her, respect her work—not just decision-making, but she's also just better at things than I am and I know and trust that.

Having deep respect is crucial, but it doesn't come easily. "The struggle with your own ego when collaborating is so hard," says Chin. "Trust is crucial to have, or else you feel you are giving more than the other person and it tears you apart. I'm great when collaborating with those who are better than me for that reason and terrible with there's no trust. Over time, you learn who can really walk the walk, and once I know I can trust them, it's for life."

In most business contexts, you can't hand-pick your team, at least not fully. And bringing along junior people is often part of the process, so many teammates may be unknowns or lack experience either in working in teams or in their particular skill set. So how do you go about establishing trust, especially when, more than likely, you aren't selecting your team from the cream of the crop of each specialty?

Trust Comes from Experience

Trust comes from the experiences that people have with one another, but, paradoxically, in order to have good experiences, you may need trust. Even if most team members don't have experience together, having even a few who do can help establish an anchor of trust and model it for others. Trusting those recommended by others you know and respect can also help. As Chin says, "I can take people sight unseen from those who are *ultra* trusted."

Another way to get through this situation is to develop genuine trust and respect among at least some of the team members to help keep everyone grounded amidst the pressure. Reid Hoffman, founder of LinkedIn, sees teams that have experience together as a competitive advantage (*http://bit.ly/2BUzjqk*) because they can often move more quickly, with quality: "Whether you're spinning through the sky at 10,000 feet, or trying to do something more grounded, there will be times when you need to build trust fast."

In *The Alliance: Managing Talent in the Networked Age* (Harvard Business Review Press), Hoffman and his coauthors describe "tours of duty" (*https://read.bi/2EEqQJO*) as a way to boost trust in an organization. Whether it's a short-term rotation where people across the organization learn about each other and build relationships or share institutional knowledge informally, or a longer-term "transformational" rotation where employees are really learning about different aspects of the business and cross-skilling to grow their careers, they say that the best way to build trust is to do work together.

Part of what happens when people have experiences together is that they develop a mutual respect for differences. Alberto Villarreal, an award-winning industrial designer who's now working on Google's mobile hardware offering of phones, tablets, and Chromebooks, says that seeing what someone is capable of —and knowing what you are capable of—is key. "I wouldn't question an electrical engineer about battery limits; they are the experts there. But we industrial designers are experts in beauty. Even if everyone has an opinion on aesthetics, at the end of the day there has to be an expert in what makes something beautiful in a way that nonexperts can't," he explains. But making yourself the authority on "beauty" takes more than a declaration. Villarreal says external indicators, such as awards or other validation from experts in the field, helps to establish his bona fides initially, but he knows that showing people his deep skill set and having others see his successes goes further than anything else. While we saw earlier the danger of giving into experts by default, there is something to be said for channeling expertise where it counts—just don't do it blindly.

Try It, You'll Like It

One of the things I consistently heard from those working at creating something new or within very tight constraints is that when a team of people trust each other, they stop arguing different perspectives based on theory. Instead, they find it faster and more productive to simply try out an idea and see if it has merit on its own. Because they've likely had the experience of trying something "crazy" together and having it work out, they are more open to trying the next crazy idea. But at the same time, teams that have tried out contentious approaches and seen them crash and burn have developed a way to shrug it off and say, "Well, maybe next time." In both cases, the experience of working through a big idea makes a team stronger.

Chin says that in the editing studio for their films, he watches Vasarhelyi and editor Bob Eisenhardt just try ideas out when they are proposed, rather than arguing about them. Vasarhelyi is such an experienced filmmaker that her intuition isn't something that she can always rationalize in the abstract. She's had the experience of trying different approaches in other settings, with other teams, and that experience transfers to new collaborations. The cumulative experience of the team gives them an advantage, even when the individuals themselves are still building up their combined experience.

Early in my career, I spent a lot of time and energy rationalizing ideas and recommendations for clients, trying to "win" an argument on principle, convinced because of my own experience that I was right. That approach not only cost me a lot of emotional energy, it probably also cost me some trust. Along the way I learned to just try out "crazy" ideas from clients, if only to have some actual, tangible thing for us to look at together. I've also had ideas that seemed *brilliant* to me as they occurred, only to find as I tried to prototype them that in fact they were *terrible*. It turns out that practice builds trust, and theory breeds argument.

Being open to trying ideas out helps build trust, but it shouldn't be confused with the real prototyping and testing that you're more likely to do once the team has decided on a direction to pursue. While doing some A/B testing of variations can tell you a lot about how different versions of the same concept perform, the disagreements that make or break trust in a team are generally more profound than variants.

If you find that your team's having unproductive disagreements over superficial things rather than more fundamental aspects, that's a good sign that they don't have a basic level of trust to depend on. And, if the team is having fundamental disagreements about strategy, core technologies, or audience needs, it might be time to take a step back.

Building Trust Through Vulnerability

Brené Brown, a research professor and best-selling author, has made a big point out of how sharing your own vulnerability makes a group stronger. She argues that perfectionism, the opposite of vulnerability, gets in the way of what we are trying to achieve: "Perfectionism is very different than self-improvement. Perfectionism is, at its core, about trying to earn approval...perfectionism is not the key to success. In fact, research shows that perfectionism hampers achievement." In a collaboration, admitting you don't know the answer actually creates more trust than insisting your theoretical knowledge is right.

But you need to cultivate vulnerability, especially if you don't hold a great deal of power or authority, to overcome the urge to be perfect and expert. You, as a proponent of successful collaboration, can create the environment for vulnerability by first being vulnerable yourself or by encouraging, or even staging, moments of weakness and introspection from senior leaders. Many executives are coached on this point and may be surprisingly open to sharing their (probably well-rehearsed and safe for consumption) weaknesses.

Sharing your weaknesses need not (and probably shouldn't) involve sharing your deepest, darkest secrets. In fact, if you aren't comfortable with the idea of being open, start small. I often make a point of throwing out terrible ideas to teams so that I can have an opportunity to admit they weren't great. That's also a chance to then praise the work of others that is stronger, thereby giving them a boost. I share stories of failures I've experienced so they can laugh with me at my mistakes and help me make more. When a group has shared the experience of making mistakes together, their reaction to being wrong or "crazy" is more likely to be a welcome moment of laughter—the best medicine.

Leading Teams Toward Trust

There are some environments where working with a broad range of people is standard operating procedure, and getting access to lots of different people isn't the challenge. Blair Reeves, Principal Product Manager for SAS, says that enterprise product management is very different, and that's the subject of his book with Benjamin Gaines, *Building Products for the Enterprise* (O'Reilly). Creating, selling, installing, and maintaining enterprise management tools inherently takes all kinds. Reeves works across several very large teams including sales, engineering, support, and more because they have a small number of large customers, compared to a company like Facebook with its massive user base. He says that at that scale, "people become small dots." The focus of product management in those two very different environments comes down to how many internal partners are needed and available.

Because the teams he oversees are already quite cross-functional and have diverse skills and perspectives, for Reeves the challenge is providing enough leadership to let others build trust in a safe space. He has to remember to remain focused on the roadmap and looking forward, using deep knowledge of the customers and industry to make a first guess at where the products should go. But he also has to be transparent about what assumptions have gone into his predictions, and be open to having the roadmap changed as the world does.

Leading teams toward trust also means not getting sucked into micromanagement. If you take your eye off the bigger picture, you'll find it hard to refocus there. You have to allow team members to use their skills and good judgment and learn to evolve them in order to build trust. As ER doctor Jon Rosenberg puts it, "I'm doing my best when I'm at 30K feet. Someone needs to keep a hold of the big picture, and not get sucked into the details." This requires a leader who is trusted, certainly, but it also requires the leader to trust the team to work through all of the moving pieces to realize the vision.

When collaborations don't have ample room between a leader and follower, or the group is chasing an unclear vision, it's obvious to people outside. Many of the negative perceptions about collaboration stem from stories of team members who aren't able to trust each other and take on roles, instead clamoring to be seen as the leader. As Nilofer Merchant, author of *The Power of Onlyness: Make Your Wild Ideas Mighty Enough to Dent the World* (Penguin), puts it (*http://bit.ly/2T8Dp91*), businesspeople sometimes perform like six-year-olds playing soccer: everyone is bunched up around the ball, following the action. Until people trust each other to do their part in the moment, no one can make a play. And this may take practice; studying soccer positions in a book or off of a whiteboard won't actually help you play them, and certainly not as a team.

Protect Trust When Things Go Wrong

And finally, with great power comes great responsibility. You can make or break trust among a team by how you act when things do go wrong. To be an effective leader of collaboration, be sure to not single out individuals to take the heat. Depending on the situation, this is a good time to treat the team as a whole and take responsibility for the mistake yourself on their behalf. You clearly don't want to shield someone from learning a valuable lesson, but at the same time, hanging a failure (that's unlikely to be one person's fault) on someone will ruin the trust not just between the two of you, but with anyone else in the team too.

Sometimes, the "failure" is one of process. The team missed a critical step, such as checking with the legal department at the right time or preserving data correctly. In these cases, it's useful to ask the team to diagnose that this happened (if it isn't already clear to them) and have them reflect on how it was missed. If it was because the team didn't value the importance of the step ahead of time, it's likely that—given a negative outcome—they better understand it now. If it was out of ignorance, ask the team to think through how they will avoid such missteps in the future. These reflection sessions should be done only with the team, not with intimidating leaders, who may miss the reflection portion of this step.

Sometimes the failure is one of product, where a solution just doesn't work. If the situation is simply that a given solution doesn't pass user testing, be sure to reframe this situation as a *success*, not a failure. As we will see in later chapters, testing ideas and having some of them not work is actually a great thing for the team to experience. But, if the failure is something that made it out into the world and led to negative consequences for those the solution was meant to help, well, that's a serious problem. In these situations, it's important to make the team understand how they let their ideas get that far without data to show how well they performed.

It's common and natural in these situations for the team to try to pin failure on one person or faction. The "I told you so" response, while natural, is not at all helpful, and you should be sure to point out that in a collaborative team, *everyone* is responsible for the outcomes. If the team disagreed about something that ultimately didn't work, dig in to understand how that disagreement didn't get resolved. It may be due to someone who is overly influential, in which case they need to acknowledge their culpability. Or, more likely, those who didn't agree fully stopped objecting at some point and gave in. I was once doing some back-country skiing, and our tests of the snow safety were pretty inconclusive. Our guide made us go around the entire group and say whether we thought we should continue or turn back. One person, who had never been outside a patrolled area before, said he didn't have a strong opinion. The guide quickly snapped, "That's not an option. When you abstain, you blame." It took quite a lot of pressure for the man to admit that he was not comfortable continuing, forcing the entire group to turn back.

As we'll discuss in future chapters, if the group can't come to a consensus, they can clearly and intentionally decide to "disagree and commit" to a direction. This means that when the group eventually realizes that the direction wasn't a good one, no one can complain, because they did *commit* to the direction, however skeptical they were of it.

As the leader, no matter what the cause of a failure or tough spot, you should focus on asking the group to understand and own the steps that led to the failure, not on the outcome or blame. The unity of the group in owning chosen solutions and sharing responsibility is the most important thing to focus on.

Troubleshooting Trust Issues

Creating a real sense of trust in the team doesn't happen overnight, and will take some support. This section offers suggestions about how to handle complications that might arise around creating and maintaining trust.

NO HISTORY OR EXPERIENCE TOGETHER

It's one thing to be producing a movie or getting the band back together and hand-picking your team from those you know well or who are the top talent in their field. But in most corporations, you don't really have that luxury. You might get to pick out a few key team members, but more often, you're working with whatever talent you've got on hand. Additionally, some teams are expressly set up to give new, or very junior, talent a place to land and be mentored by those who have more experience with the company and in their field.

While it's true that the best way to get trust is to give it, it's not particularly helpful when crunch time comes and the pressure mounts. No amount of good intentions makes up for knowing how someone will act in a given situation, or what their strengths and weaknesses are.

So what can I do?

Land an anchor tenant

Advocate for someone you have experience with to be on the team. This seed of trust can be a springboard for others. If you are new, or don't have a connection that you can pull into the collaboration, find two or three people who do have experience together to be on the team. Their trust will serve as the anchor just as well. Trust doesn't have to start or come from you alone.

Start small

If you've got a rag-tag bunch of misfits that don't know one another, think about smaller, low-risk things you can start on together to learn where each other's strengths and limits lie.

Start with related teams

Likely, one of the biggest collaboration challenges your organization faces is getting two different teams to share their thinking and work about related issues. One way to break down walls is to simply start sharing work and questions between teams, without trying to coordinate workstreams.

As each group begins to appreciate what the other knows and doesn't know, you can start building shared trust to actually align efforts better.

Hire outside consultants to supplement your team

Hiring outside consultants who are likely to have some experience together can help you model what you eventually expect from your internal team. Make sure that the outside experts don't dominate a team or cause those with less experience and trust to just follow blindly.

Help people opt in

You don't have to wait for the powers that be to assemble a supergroup for you. If you begin sharing aspects of what you are working on, and what problem you are trying to solve, you may find people actually offering and asking to be a part of the effort. These folks will likely have an easier time earning and giving trust because of their intrinsic motivations and will focus on the end goal over established lines of authority.

MICROMANAGING FROM ABOVE

If there's one thing I personally find hard to handle, it's when someone makes their mistrust as clear as day by constantly meddling in my affairs from a position of authority. It's the number one thing I try never to do to others, even if it means biting my fingernails for a bit. If you've been on the receiving end of well-intentioned but unwelcome attention from a superior, you know the frustration that comes from wanting to prove yourself capable and not really having the chance. When those above us in the food chain don't give adequate space for us to prove ourselves, we end up in a negative cycle where no trust can be established and so none is given. If your team is being micromanaged, it's likely not because there's a complete lack of trust. It may be happening out of a fear of failure that the micromanager is making a self-fulfilling prophecy. Or, sometimes there's concern about a specific person that the manager is trying to mitigate.

So what can I do?

Give them something to focus on

Just as Thorsten Borek suggests for dealing with leaders (as we discussed in Chapter 1), give micromanagers an important job to do. Asking your boss for "help" signals your respect for their authority, and gives them an outlet for nervous energy. Asking them to lead sessions, share their subject-matter expertise, or plan activities are all ways to channel their focus away from individuals.

Overcommunicate

One way to occupy micromanagers is with a flood of information and requests for advice and decisions. By giving a lot of information, you are feeding their desire to know what's going on and helping reduce the tendency to lash out when they are surprised.

MISTRUST WITHIN THE TEAM

If you have someone who doesn't seem to trust the team, they may act out by stubbornly refusing to engage, or by contributing a negative running commentary about the effort. Or, you may have one person on the receiving end of the mistrust, rather than the whole team. This can be very destructive to the team, and excruciating for the target(s). It's not always obvious why the mistrust is surfacing, since many times, it's irrational. In my experience that person's mistrust is based on their own insecurity, rather than any real, tangible issue. Occasionally, the mistrust is historical, based on a prior bad experience together. In either case, it's crucial you nip it in the bud.

Sometimes the internal mistrust comes up when it's time to get "work" done and produce artifacts or research findings. Brainstorming and being open-minded feel less risky and is less constrained than producing results, and it's understandable that some will get nervous. Once people have started to mix it up with each other, being exposed to new ways of thinking, one person starts developing opinions about the next lane over and just can't keep it to themselves. Other times, someone who feels they are carrying a bigger share of the load can take it upon themselves to "load level" in an unproductive way. They may begin trying to control what others do or shirking their own responsibilities.

So what can I do?

Weed out bad blood

When mistrust is based on prior bad experience, it's worth sitting one or both people down and asking them to put it aside. Better still is to ferret out the issue ahead of time by doing "reference checks" about previous experiences. Regardless of whether you learn that bad blood exists in the moment or ahead of time, however, I suggest you meet with one or both parties to clear the air. If you sense that the mistrust runs very deep, consider removing one of the parties. While someone may have incredible expertise that the team needs, if they won't share it, it's not useful. You can invite them in on a part-time basis in order to harness their expertise without exposing the team to the negative effects of mistrust.

Swap work

When individuals start to act out because they think they're doing more than their fair share, try having team members swap each other's work in a session. This most often happens when one person's domain is more "technical" than another's. But this distinction is a false one. While it's true that everyone can write by pressing keys on a keyboard, writing clearly and persuasively takes as much experience and skill as writing code, but in today's business world the chauvinism about engineering being somehow harder than other aspects of the work is a fatal trap. After all, Apple's break-through with the iPod wasn't (only) due to the six lines of text and a click wheel to play music; the tagline "1,000 songs in your pocket" did much to set it apart from the other portable hard drives with headphone jacks on the market at the time. Obviously you aren't going to make a marketing expert write code, or have data scientists write copy, at least not in "production." But you can have the group tackle these different aspects of the work together, (briefly) describing in the abstract what a good algorithm would enable, and what would make a good tagline for the end product.

Conclusion

Trust is a critical ingredient in healthy teams. It helps them overcome adversity and be more open to sharing ideas and testing them out to make them stronger. But trust isn't something that can be installed in the team—it comes from experience that people have together and needs time and space to develop. You can help by finding or recruiting people who have a level of trust already established to seed the team and model what trust looks like. It's also important that leaders stay focused at the right level, keeping the big picture in mind, and let teams learn and grow to develop that trust, especially when things go wrong.

Key Takeaways

- Trust isn't something that can be installed in a team; it comes from experience working together and learning each other's strengths and weaknesses.

- When trust happens, team members are more open to trying ideas out rather than debating them or relying on hierarchy to resolve disputes.

- Being vulnerable with one another about struggles and concerns is a great way to build trust.

- Building trust takes time to develop in a safe space; leaders can support this by getting teams to reflect on root causes and share responsibility for backlash when things go wrong.

4

Make Space

Working closely together means just that—getting close. As we've discussed in previous chapters, when we bring a variety of people together, we need to think about who we will invite and how we will operate. But just as important is the actual space in which we collaborate. In this chapter we look at the idea of using "space," both physical and virtual, in a collaboration to support the team. For many offices, collaborative work is very different than what typically goes on, so you should be intentional about making space work for you and your team members.

While many teams must and do work together remotely (i.e., in distributed locations), many people believe there's really no substitute for being in the same room, though I've certainly run into people who feel that remote working is as good as, if not better than, being colocated. On a *Freakonomics* podcast about Harvard's study of open plan offices, Janet Pogue McLaurin, an expert in global workspaces, says that studies show that up to 50% of our work is actually heads-down focused time, with 25% of our time being spent face-to-face, and the rest being virtual. She says that all of this points to the need for teams to have some choice about their spaces, to allow for both quality time with colleagues and space to think and work. Many find that being colocated allows for "spontaneous collaboration," where people encounter each other and share information organically. Whether you work in the same space and time or are distributed, though, there are ways you can help your teams by structuring the "places" where work happens.

Working with Physical Space

Jorge Arango, an information architect, says the spaces in which he works with collaborators need to be crafted, rather than taken for granted. He tries, whenever possible, to get teams out of their day-to-day buildings into new settings that don't hold unseen agendas and pet ideas. He says, "The space becomes the canvas for ideas; the room itself becomes the artifact" that the whole group has created and knows inside out. "Notes need to live on walls, not trapped in notebooks, to become useful," he finds. "Space needs to help people escape the 'tyranny of spoken language' where a third way between competing ideas can emerge."

It's not just about exposing notes and ideas, though. Arango finds that people develop a spatial memory of where ideas and assumptions are in a room. And this isn't accidental. Arango constantly grooms the space to organize the ideas that are generated and synthesized within it. While the space itself can't serve as the true end artifact, it can be powerful during the period where a focused, dedicated team is working through unresolved issues.

Physical spaces shouldn't be kept *too* groomed, however. The adage about a messy desk signaling a brilliant mind may actually have some truth to it, at least where collaborations are concerned. Teams that have their own space to keep things visible and mutable for a period of time are better able to keep their minds and options open, because they can see raw data such as customer quotes or brainstormed concepts side-by-side, which helps them think laterally. Thinking laterally means that they aren't trying to derive the answer analytically, but instead are more open to ideas and co-creation.

If possible, getting a space set up for a few weeks (or whatever duration your team is exploring and selecting solutions) can be very helpful. This allows the team to have a safe space to work together that they come to know well.

Leaders can also benefit from having access to teams in their space and relating to them in person. Tom Chi, formerly of GoogleX, describes how he changed up his office seating as a manager at Yahoo, where typically management sat together, away from their employees. Instead, his office was ringed by rows of developers and designers whose skills he could tap with little effort. When he ran into a challenge that he wanted to develop solutions for, he could call out to the group to see who was available and quickly assemble a team to prototype approaches. Catherine Courage, a VP of Ads and Payments at Google, manages a huge group that is distributed worldwide. She makes a point to visit teams a few times a year because it's so valuable to have a less formal, unscheduled period to interact.

Too Much Togetherness

When "collaboration" is constant, it's probably not actually happening. Often companies will throw everyone into an open floor plan and watch as they retreat into sending emails to just keep their heads clear. Space isn't all about the big group working face-to-face, it's also getting time to focus on your own. In Harvard's study of open office plans (*https://hbs.me/2GPqSAP*), researcher Ethan Bernstein found that when space is too open it negatively affects productivity, as people seek to have some sense of privacy and time to focus. The secret to helping groups collaborate is to allow for them to come together in a safe, familiar area where everyone can see the evolution of the group's work over time. But it also involves letting people retreat back to their own working space regularly to do "work," whether that's administrative tasks or working heads-down on the team's ideas to flesh them out or capture details to share with others in the future.

It is extremely helpful to have a regular schedule and cadence to using the shared space. At two consultancies I've worked for, Cooper and frog design, teams would often spend the morning together, when everyone is fresh, to work through their ideas for a few hours. Then, afternoons were dedicated to working solo or in smaller pairs on more tactical items. Make sure not only that teams get their focus time, but also that it's predictable and understood, perhaps enshrined in team norms, so that your colleagues don't get antsy.

Working with Virtual Spaces

Remote working is a controversial topic among the experts I spoke with. Stanford professor Nicholas Bloom ran a two-year study that found remote work could actually boost productivity by reducing commute times and allowing people to have time to focus, not to mention saving money on office space. But another study, by Joseph Grenny and David Maxfield, found that remote workers felt "left out" when they weren't close to the action. What appears to be a common thread is that when people aren't colocated, it takes attention to make sure they're connecting in unstructured and spontaneous ways—which they can do by using tools well. The Stanford study also found that not everyone enjoyed the experience of working remotely. Supporting people's preferences around where to work, if possible, can help.

There is also debate over, and individual preferences for, synchronous versus asynchronous communication through tools like video calls and shared documents. Matt LeMay, author of *Agile for Everybody* (O'Reilly), described using shared documents as especially challenging. "Asynchronous communication is ruining everything," he told me. But, at the same time, you can't take colocation and synchronous communication for granted. And, as LeMay points out, being colocated doesn't guarantee high-quality synchronous communication, either.

John Maeda, on the other hand, says even when teams are face-to-face, relying on asynchronous commenting on a shared document is preferable (*http://bit.ly/2EBWCGZ*). He's in the camp that believes that when people are remote, you should capitalize on their ability to take in and provide information on their own time. As we saw in earlier chapters, not everyone likes and is good at the intense face-to-face discussions where decisions get hashed out. By using virtual tools, you may get a higher-quality discussion from the group.

Remote work does appear to be a growing trend. As we make products and services that help users worldwide access information and benefits 24/7 and on the go, employees have begun to demand the same flexibility for themselves. Whether it's helping working parents time-shift work to allow for child care, or supporting those who prefer to skip a long commute in favor of working at home, or international teams working on an objective, we can and should have ways to adapt our collaborative work. Given the divergence in opinions about working synchronously versus asynchronously, it may be worth doing a specific test of each approach and letting the group determine what works best for them.

VIRTUAL SPACES AREN'T JUST FOR DISTRIBUTED TEAMS

Even if a team is colocated for much of the time, there are also limitations to actually working together *synchronously*. Especially for those whose calendars are overloaded, finding the time and space to meet face-to-face can become a real impediment to teamwork. Virtual spaces are great for supporting those who are separated not just by place, but also by time.

Being able to maximize the real-time interactions that a team has is key, says Vanessa Cho of Google Ventures. In her former role leading a team of 200 people across seven locations working on Google apps like Calendar, Gmail, and Drive, she found herself needing to collapse time and space in impossible ways to bring everyone together. She and her team eventually found ways to work within the limits of the laws of physics, using the very tools they were working on.

Certainly the tools we have to support remote collaboration have improved over the years. From the ability to edit documents together in real time, to Slack, to conference calls with video components, a great deal of what a team needs is accessible when people aren't colocated.

But we've all cursed the seemingly required 10 minutes of battling the dial-in system at the beginning of a meeting and wished we could all just get together and hash things out in person. Given the boon that supporting remote work is to teams, it's worth spending the time and energy to get your virtual space game on point.

Troubleshooting (Physical and Virtual) Space Issues

There are steps you can take to create spaces that support collaboration. This section provides suggestions about how to get physical and virtual spaces working for you and the team.

NO CONSISTENT SPACE AVAILABLE

In every office setting I've seen, space is at a premium. And most spaces are often barely functional for modern ways of working. Spaces that groups of people can work in effectively can be especially hard to come by. Having a dedicated space over time is a luxury not everyone can afford. But there are ways that you can set up, maintain, and break down spaces that will help your team capitalize on the benefits of a shared physical space, even when conditions aren't ideal.

So what can I do?

Get a temporary space
Use a regular conference room or other large area to hold a workshop for a few hours or a day or two. If possible, renting a space takes advantage of the fact that the space is unfamiliar and gets people out of their normal routines.

Take it to go
When you have to leave the space you've created together, you need not leave it *all* behind. Large Post-its (2×3 feet) are the best tool for facilitating groups in a temporary space; using them to collect insights and ideas lets you transport aspects of a physical space back into the team's natural habitat. Just make sure that when you move the work, the team helps with organizing and storing it so that the new mental model is imprinted on everyone.

LACK OF ENGAGEMENT DURING REMOTE MEETINGS

When everyone can't be in the same place at the same time, it may be a challenge to keep everyone as engaged as you'd like. You might notice that some people are not following along, and when you can't see them, you may not know why. A few tactical changes can help you know what's going on with your audience and make the proceedings easier to follow.

So what can I do?

Be a "host"

Think about a working session or demo as a type of TV show you're hosting. Don't just focus on one thing. If the discussion is around the table or at the whiteboard, show the room and whiteboard using a positionable camera. Even if you're all reviewing a shared document, you can break away from that screen periodically to bring everyone back together into the discussion rather than staring at the slides or document.

Be specific

One of the complaints I've heard from those working remotely, especially when many people are in a room together, is that they get lost about what's being discussed. Get people in the room to speak explicitly, naming the thing they're talking about rather than saying "this here," and make sure to ask for understanding and input from remote participants. As a facilitator, you can and should break in from time to time to remind those in the room that there are others who aren't there and may need additional context.

Be early

Remote meetings always go wrong at the outset. Dial-ins don't work, and people need to be wrangled. Get set up ahead of time, dialing in early to work out the kinks, at least until it becomes routine (if it ever does).

LARGE GROUP MEETINGS DON'T FEEL COLLABORATIVE

Wrangling a large group to come together and generate or evaluate ideas can be a challenge. I find that when the audience gets over 7–10 people, it takes a ton of effort to actually get people participating. One reason for this might be because being in a large group can mean people don't know one another well. It may also be because large groups generally come together to *receive information*, not participate.

Whatever the cause, there are times when it just makes sense to get a large group together. You may need to get several camps to understand the problem or share their perspectives. Perhaps you want to tap into lots of different expertise and get them building off of each other, and that means you need to use the space well.

So what can I do?

Prepare

It's going to take some choreography to get people moving around the space. Think through different areas of the room for different activities. Work in groups and have each one use a different part of the room, and then switch the groups around so that people can work more closely but still get exposure to the entire group.

Provide ample standing room

You'll need people to be able to navigate the space, take in ideas, and even place and group ideas themselves. This requires clear space to move around.

Make sure there's sufficient seating

While you want people on their feet, they can't stand the whole time. Make sure you have seats for everyone, even if the chairs need to be moved in and out, or around, the room. In some cultures there are specific seats or positions that the boss occupies. Whether it's the head of the table or a specific chair, shake things up by assigning seats and grouping people in different ways.

Consider your writing surfaces

If you need people to contribute written ideas, whether by writing on Post-its or sketching solutions, think about what they will write on. If possible, avoid having a big conference table; instead, use smaller tables or individual surfaces so people aren't wedged apart or tempted to open their laptops and check out.

Clear some wall space

Jorge Arango's advice to make things visible requires wall space. Whether you put up big Post-its or use whiteboards, be sure to create and label clear places where different parts of the conversation are recorded. Large foam-core boards, which let you carry the work around, are also useful. Keeping tidy isn't as important as keeping organized. Good facilitators will use clear headings and colors to designate different topics, approaches, or hypotheses that the team can internalize.

Pay attention to mood

It can be useful to control the mood—for example, by dimming the lights or playing music when you want people to work independently on developing or critiquing ideas. Changing the mood when you want to group to reconvene sends a clear signal that you've switched into a different mode.

Don't forget food

Low blood sugar can make people cranky, and breaking for meals may have your team wandering off. Feeding people during a meeting or taking the whole team out to eat is a great way to make room for people to socialize and get to know one another while sustaining them.

Conclusion

The physical and virtual spaces we work in can affect how well we collaborate, so it's worth putting in some effort to optimize them. Physical spaces help people have higher-bandwidth interactions and create a spatial mental map of the ideas generated within them. But while it's useful to be able to come back to a space and have impressions and memories of discussions, it isn't always an option for teams that aren't colocated or can't always find time to be together. Virtual spaces allow for more asynchronous communications and support distributed teams. However, they can be difficult to get working right. It's not necessarily that one option is better than the other, but people have different preferences for how they work and it's important to support those whenever possible. It's also important to supply spaces where folks not only can be together, but also can focus independently on their work, whether in person or remotely.

Key Takeaways

- The space that a team works in is critical to the effort. It provides literal and figurative space where ideas can live, and helps teams create a mental map of what's been explored and discussed.

- Physical spaces have the advantage of giving people a spatial model of the work, and support face-to-face communication that is high-bandwidth.

- Virtual spaces support asynchronous communication and distributed teams who can't rely on in-person communication.

- People need space to work in a "heads-down" manner, not just in a group brainstorm setting.

- Provide choices about whether people meet up in person or virtually to allow for differences in how people prefer to work.

PART II

Setting Clear Direction

Collaboration that drives new solutions means being open to different ideas and perspectives, but that openness requires structure to keep it from getting messy and going off the rails. When the answer you seek isn't obvious, group dynamics and corporate culture can get in the way. This part discusses principles to plan out your collaboration and set clear objectives for the team to help you know where you're going, and know when you get there.

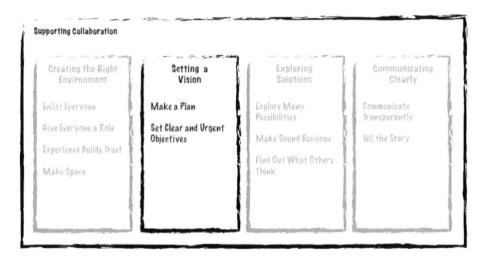

Supporting Collaboration

Creating the Right Environment	Setting a Vision	Exploring Solutions	Communicating Clearly
Enlist Everyone	Make a Plan	Explore Many Possibilities	Communicate Transparently
Give Everyone a Role	Set Clear and Urgent Objectives	Make Sound Decisons	Tell the Story
Experience Builds Trust		Find Out What Others Think	
Make Space			

5

Make a Plan

One misconception about collaboration is that it's a freewheeling effort where teams are encouraged to work free from rules and processes that might constrain them. It's tempting, especially when the problem has a number of unknowns, to just get the group together and dive in, because it's true that we want individuals freed to participate. But the effort? That takes planning. In this chapter, we'll look at ways to provide the right amount and kind of structure to help teams focus and avoid interpersonal clashes that arise out of stress. Structure comes from the natural cycle of idea development, and from establishing clear periods of time to start, complete, and reflect on work. Providing a plan to stakeholders also helps give the team enough cover to actually do work instead of fending off questions about when they will be done.

Creating a plan simply means stating what you think will happen, what steps you think are needed, and some idea of how long things will take. It's common for some people to shun this step, because there's often no way to know ahead of time what will happen and when. I emphasize with those I coach that when planning, you're just making your best guess at what will happen, and as the person closest to the situation, your guess is probably better than anyone else's. Creating a plan isn't about controlling every step of the process, especially when the situation is complex and unpredictable. To help teams maintain focus, take some time to spell out what you think will happen. As Dwight Eisenhower once said, "In preparing for battle I have always found that plans are useless, but planning is indispensable."

Planning helps teams make productive use of their time and sets expectations without being overly directive. In researching this book, I observed two elementary school classrooms where teachers with different levels of experience ran group projects to teach collaboration. The groups were to create a play to perform at a school assembly where the theme was collaboration. While both classrooms were loud, with many children speaking and moving around at once—some writing dialog, others creating dance routines—I noticed a big difference between the groups based on how the teacher set up the assignment. One teacher asked the children to self-organize into groups and create a play to teach the younger students what collaboration is and why it's useful. The other teacher, one with more experience with this exercise, divided kids into groups and described the play they were to make. She also had them plan out how they would spend their time to create their masterpieces.

The kids with less structure did complete the assignment, for the most part, but with interesting side effects. Some children, given the chance to self-select into a group, chose not to join. One child, who tended toward the shyer side, said, "I'm collaborating with myself. It's way easier." The child's natural aversion to chaos led him to not participate since he couldn't see any way to bring order to the task. The groups that didn't create plans for how to use their time had too little structure to keep them focused on the *goal* of the exercise. Their performances had a lot of energy and funny in-jokes, but weren't fully understandable to the audience. A few kids told me they were nervous and wished they didn't have to perform, worrying that the other students would laugh at them. In contrast, the kids that had structured their time were more confident in their performances and positive about working together.

Planning your collaborative work isn't about making Gantt charts or deadlines, but rather structuring the time you have and tracking progress toward the overall goal of the effort. To develop this structure, you should understand the risks and consequences that you're facing and align expectations about where you'll be at different points in time. The plans you develop with the team should be made visible and revisited frequently, so that they serve their function as guidance for the team rather than a prescriptive set of steps to follow.

In this chapter, we'll look at how ideas grow from initial sparks into more fully formed concepts and concrete solutions. Along the way, you will need to understand and manage the risks and unknowns your team will face, and plan to mitigate them. By structuring the team's time and thinking to test ideas out, run experiments, and gather data, you help them stay open to different perspectives while being grounded in the real issues that could harm the effort.

How Ideas Develop

Providing structure starts with understanding how ideas develop. I offer an adaptation of the "double diamond" approach, created by the Design Council in the

UK, which structures efforts around *divergent* thinking, where the team loosens constraints and generates many options, and *convergent* thinking, where the team specifies criteria to select ideas and try them out. The process of being expansive and critical repeats as you learn more and bring new information back to the challenge to inform another round of work. The "double diamond" refers to the fact that teams can use this approach in a first pass for determining objectives, and in a second for developing solutions. Since I find that both of those activities often take more than one cycle, I've depicted it as a single diamond that can be applied to either understanding a problem or developing solutions (see Figure 5-1). The diagram shows the cycle and the key inflection points that you should be aware of to lead people through it effectively. It has four basic stages:

Set objectives
Where the problem to be solved is stated, and success criteria are set

Explore
Where diverse solutions to ideas are generated

Decide
Where solutions are evaluated critically and one is selected to be tested

Test and learn
Where solutions are tested and data is gathered to evaluate and learn how to improve

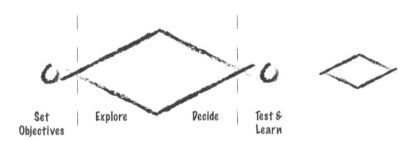

Set Objectives | Explore | Decide | Test & Learn

Figure 5-1. How ideas develop

The diamond shape alludes to the creative process mentioned earlier, where you are channeling energies to be either divergent (many options are explored) or convergent (criteria are used to select options to try out). What's key is structuring activities to understand what you're trying to solve for, giving the team time to explore, being disciplined about choosing what to pursue, and trying it out.

This structure helps teams focus on the problem and solution, and know when to be critical and when to be expansive in their thinking.

Often, without active coaching or facilitation, teams will attempt to skip to the end of this process by developing the obvious solution rather than trying different approaches. Because the value of collaboration is to bring many different perspectives to bear on a problem, and not assume we know the answer to complex questions, you should help your teams avoid this tendency by planning out time and being intentional about when you are diverging and converging together.

I've seen many teams be especially challenged during the exploration stage where they have spent time understanding a problem and begun developing solutions, but haven't landed on anything tangible yet. Providing stakeholders with progress updates here is tricky because there isn't a satisfying conclusion to report, and confidence about how the work is going is low. Being transparent in your plan about how your teams are using time will help to manage stakeholders' expectations and push back against pressure to "just deliver something."

Plan to Experiment and Reduce Risks

Because collaboration can help with situations where there's a lot of unknowns, it can be useful to plan for time to investigate and "de-risk" situations, not just create solutions. It's worth asking, how much risk is there in finding the solution, or how possible is it that you'll develop ideas that fail? And, if you do fail, how bad are the consequences for the users and the company?

One way to think about the output of your collaboration is to frame it as being either an *experiment*, where you try a variety of ideas in a safe space to learn how they might perform and ferret out any unknowns without exposing yourself to negative outcomes, or a *launch*, where you release things into the real world to learn more specifically how they perform (see Figure 5-2).

Experiment

Launch

Figure 5-2. Sometimes you want to test ideas in a controlled experiment versus a launch

For example, when I was part of a team designing a robotic surgical system, we would run experiments weekly or daily, by creating a simulation of the doctor's controls and display to understand how well different approaches worked without involving the actual robot, which took a lot of time and money to prepare. Our experiments were about building confidence around a specific idea, or learning what made another idea fail. The environment we ran them in was highly controlled, with low risk of catastrophe if we were wrong. We didn't always try to make the environment realistic, either. In one case we had doctors race each other on the system as a way of seeing many different challenges quickly, even though in reality, speed is never the key factor. Other times, with versions we felt strongly about, we would conduct trials on cadavers, or even animals, to validate certain choices. The decision to operate on a cadaver or animal was sufficiently serious that the team would choose this option only when we had a high level of confidence in what we were learning.

A launch, on the other hand, is when you actually put your solution out into the world, with factors you can't control and effects that are real. Whether you're sending shoppers to a new checkout process or collecting important data in a new way, there's a possibility that if (really, when) things go wrong, the effects aren't confined to the lab. But just because a launch goes out into the world and escapes the controls doesn't mean you have no way to manage the risks and downsides of failures. The simplest option is to limit the scope of those using it to a small group. This can help unearth problems in the details that are likely easy to address once you know what they are. Another mitigation is to keep redundant processes in place while you try out a new one. For example, at PG&E when we released apps for the workforce to use to inspect equipment, we kept the old paper processes in place for a few months so we could compare the two sets of data we collected to make sure we were getting the same, correct data with the new tools.

By understanding how complicated your problem space and solution space is, you can figure out how broadly you should cast your net when developing ideas. You can visualize this as the intersection of risk (i.e., the chance that you'll choose a bad solution) and consequences (i.e., the material damage done by mistakes or inaction), as shown in Figure 5-3.

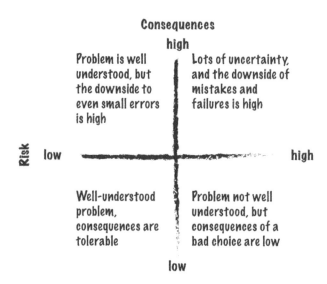

Figure 5-3. Mapping out complications versus risk in your effort helps you plan

Figure 5-4 shows how teams can manage risks and consequences by structuring their time in the form of experiments and launches to try things out and understand how well proposed solutions work.

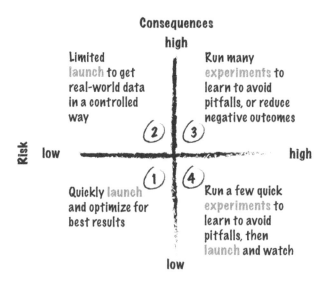

Figure 5-4. Connecting risk and consequences to experiments and launches

When you are dealing with ideas in the lower left, quadrant 1, there's very little chance that you will choose a poor solution, and if you do, the consequences are low, so you may not have to spend very long looking for a breakthrough idea. Likely there are well-known patterns you can learn from and test out. For example, driving traffic to a new feature may take a few A/B tests to work out specific wording or color choices, but it won't cause catastrophe if you haven't yet optimized it.

On the other hand, if you face a high risk of not finding a good solution and the consequences are dire, as they are in the upper right (quadrant 3), you'll need to do enough exploration to drive down that risk and uncover some insights to learn what makes better or worse solutions. For example, creating a new heads-up display for use in mining operations has safety and cost concerns that mean you'll need to take time to test out what works and/or learn how to reduce the negative consequences of mistakes with safety implications.

Most collaborations are likely to find themselves in the other two quadrants. Something that has high risk, in that no comparable solutions have been identified, but won't have a ruinous effect if it fails (quadrant 4) can be explored quickly by the team, because you can move to testing with the audience to get "real-world" data about what's working. For example, developing early capabilities that can augment a product offering might be worth the team spending a few cycles "dogfooding," or working out kinks, before launching to customers in a trial.

If you're looking at a problem with serious consequences, but where the path to a solution isn't risky (quadrant 2), you'll want to try out ideas in a safe space for a bit longer. For example, rolling out changes to an ecommerce pipeline might affect sales numbers, and rolling out a sweeping policy for a part of HR operations might affect retention and morale. Both of the areas are well understood, so the risk of making a mistake is low, but if you do there will be major consequences.

So, when thinking about how broadly you want the team to look for solutions, consider how well understood the problem space is versus the consequences of failure. Working in an incremental fashion—that is, testing out ideas as you go—helps you avoid implementing a terrible solution, and acknowledges that any solution over time will be refined and optimized for a better return. By balancing efforts to think expansively and efforts to drive down risk, you can develop a plan that will help align your stakeholders in terms of how long the effort will take, and why. This is also useful information to periodically revisit with outside stakeholders to show incremental progress when you don't have a big reveal.

Keep in mind that these models are intended to be used transparently, with the group evaluating and deciding the details of the plan together. Resist the temptation of keeping these models to yourself to create a plan and then asking the team to sign on. The team's trust and buy-in will be strengthened when you all develop plans together. And when those plans change—as they will—it's easier for the group to adjust when everyone's got the same background. The sidebar "Planning Your Effort and Understanding Complexity" shows more specifically how you can lead a group to think through the approach together.

Tools to Help Plan Your Collaboration: Planning Your Effort and Understanding Complexity

Planning out efforts for problems that are complex and ambiguous is tricky. The first place to start is by deciding just how complex and ambiguous your problem is. Have the team think through what they know, and what they've learned, about the problem and possible outcomes.

Here are some questions that can help you determine how complicated your challenges are:

- Are there comparable problems/solutions that exist to use as a starting point?

- Is the problem well understood, based on data, or are there only assumptions that need testing?

- What's the worst-case scenario if a solution goes wrong? What's at stake?

- Can effects and outcomes be scaled down and tested on a smaller population to reduce negative consequences while we learn what works?

This exercise can also be done periodically as you learn more, to help the team see how and if they are de-risking the situation with new information.

Example Plans to Manage Risks and Consequences

You can use the framework in Figure 5-5 to determine how many rounds you'll need to diverge and converge with stakeholders to minimize risk, weed out uncertainty, and create trust. Depending on how complex your problem space is, you can set aside the time needed and communicate that to stakeholders as a matter of mitigating exposure to negative consequences, rather than meeting arbitrary deadlines.

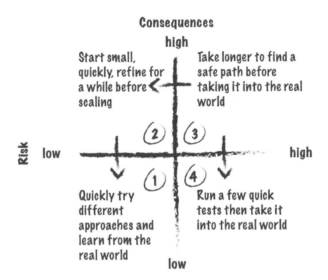

Figure 5-5. Plan to de-risk and manage negative outcomes in your project by moving it from situations with higher risks and consequences to those with fewer risks and consequences

Being in the upper left or lower right means that you should budget two to three cycles to reduce risk or uncertainty and set expectations that the answer is unlikely to happen right away. Once you've worked through a few approaches, you can take a cycle to create something that you can test more thoroughly.

Now let's look at a few example collaboration plans for different scenarios.

LOW RISK, LOW CONSEQUENCES

Because this is a well-understood problem with little downside, you can do quick passes to develop ideas to then test with as real an audience as you can get (Figure 5-6). If you are in a position to run A/B tests, your collaboration simply becomes a bit of structure around an iterative development process; maybe you're working in a "sprint ahead" mode where the exploration and testing is done ahead of when it is to be implemented.

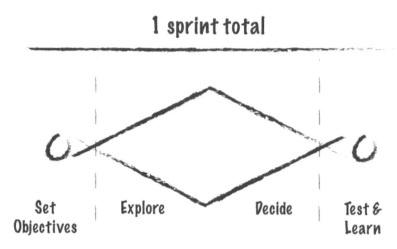

1 sprint total

Set Objectives | **Explore** | **Decide** | **Test & Learn**

Figure 5-6. An example for low-risk, low-consequence efforts

This might also apply to more organizational challenges like trying flexible seating arrangements or improving internal communications about an HR processes.

LOW RISK, HIGH CONSEQUENCES

When you are in the top-left quadrant, dealing with something that's pretty well understood but with big potential downsides, you'll want to slow down the process to make sure you're getting really sound information about the effects, intended and unintended, of your solution (Figure 5-7). In this case, you'll want to make sure you've defined the context and objectives fully, giving the team time to understand and clearly articulate them. Then, you can explore and develop a few tests that you run for long enough to get a good trend from the data. This could apply to rolling out a new travel and expense policy, where you want to make sure you've worked out kinks before asking the whole company to use it. The goal of this type of effort is to drive down the negative consequences by optimizing what works with some protection.

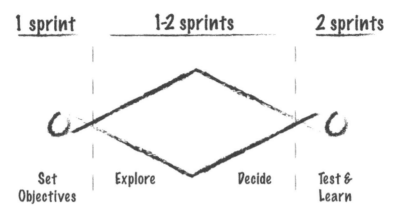

Figure 5-7. An example for low-risk, high-consequence efforts

An example of a situation that's relatively low risk but high consequence is changing a checkout flow for a highly trafficked ecommerce site, where the factors involved are well understood and there are other case studies to consult, but if a mistake happens it could have a big impact on revenues.

HIGH RISK, LOW CONSEQUENCES

In this quadrant are efforts that don't have a big downside to them but do have a lot of uncertainty about what will create the desired results. When you have a great idea but no sense of what it will take to pull it off, or if you want to innovate new ideas, it's good to set aside a few cycles within the team's whitespace to work through both wild and mundane ideas and shore up the team's understanding of where the constraints really are (Figure 5-8). From there, testing the best ideas to get external input is useful. The goal of this engagement is to drive down the risk while keeping the consequences low.

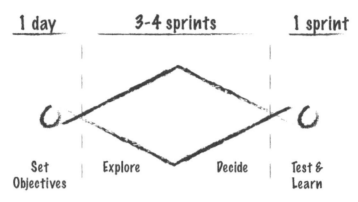

1 day	3-4 sprints		1 sprint

Set Objectives   Explore   Decide   Test & Learn

Figure 5-8. An example for high-risk, low-consequence efforts

An example of such a situation might be developing a radical new offering for an audience where the team doesn't have many points of reference to learn from, but their efforts won't threaten existing revenues or customer loyalty. Launching new features that augment a product or service but don't take away its current capabilities is worth experimenting with, since you won't have to worry about killing your core offering.

HIGH RISK, HIGH CONSEQUENCES

In this situation, your focus should be to either/both drive down the risk and uncertainty about what will work, or to drive down the consequences of a misstep. It is helpful to spend a sprint thoroughly defining the problem and sharing what everyone knows about the territory, but then it's better to actually move into the territory and start exploring. You can then run single-sprint-long cycles that let you test ideas quickly (Figure 5-9). At any point you can stop and assess what you've learned. This type of work should be done outside the cadence of a shipping development team or operational team. This team needs to be able to share their findings with senior leaders and communicate clearly about how they are progressing in the face of a lot of risk and no tangible benefits.

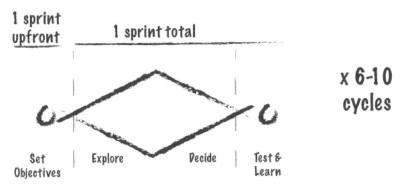

Figure 5-9. An example plan for high-risk, high-consequence efforts

Making changes to the tax code is an example of where there isn't a straight path to follow toward desired outcomes, and if something goes wrong it affects a lot of people.

Timeboxing Over Deadlines

One way to deal with the pressure to get to the answer quickly and short-circuit the process is *timeboxing*, or defining a set amount of time for an activity versus a specific outcome. This helps keep the momentum of the team going, and get them trying out ideas to gain feedback and data about what works to show progress instead of jumping to the end.

Years ago, a group of artist friends introduced me to figure drawing. They had set up a tableau and a model, and I was interested, but anxious. After all, I'm no artist! But as we got started, one of them described how this was going to work. We'd start out with three or four sketches of 10 seconds each. From there we'd move on to 30-second drawings and minute-long drawings until finally, at the end, we'd have a full 10 minutes to draw the model. I was instantly curious. Ten seconds?! That was barely enough time to pick up my pencil and make a line or two! So that's what I did. The 10 seconds was the constraint I'd been given, so there was only so much detail and "quality" my drawing could have.

The same thing happens with teamwork. It can be tempting to hang back from making decisions, especially if the group isn't in deep agreement, burning valuable time trying to satisfy a need for information or perfection that just isn't possible. Vanessa Cho of Google Ventures is a big fan of "time chunking," and she says it's often saved her in situations where the time pressure feels overwhelming. By setting up shorter, more limited sections of time, you can often satisfy the need to keep things moving and show progress, without trying to solve for every unknown you face.

"You can't just go on forever," Cho says. "But I also want everyone involved to know that while we are moving forward, we aren't done." She points out that to be successful, timeboxing must be very explicit and made transparent to everyone. You may want to just timebox a stage in the process, or run the entire cycle as a single sprint, working fast and loose to see what gets unstuck. What's key is that you don't skip stages or squish them too far. And, when you reach the end of your timebox, you can always add "extra time" if you aren't *quite* finished.

How Many Cycles Do I Need?

The question that most teams and their stakeholders ask themselves early and often is "How long is this going to take?" The answer to this question is, of course, the annoying "it depends," but there are some ways to look at your problem to give yourself some guidelines. Obviously problems and environments will differ, so you should apply your own judgment to arrive at a final plan, but these exercises will give you some lenses to consider instead of making arbitrary guesses or engaging in wishful thinking.

The first assumption is that you are working in *sprints*, or defined cycles of effort that repeat. Even if you aren't following Agile practices, it's useful to frame your work in cycles so that you can communicate increments of progress outside the team while maintaining some whitespace for the core team to work in that feels safe.

You can choose whether your sprints are one or two weeks long, but for my purposes in this chapter I'll assume you're working in one-week sprints. *The shortest time to set aside for a collaboration is one sprint.* This is not to say you can't do quick workshops in a day, or even do a whole cycle in a few days, but if you are working on a specific challenge with rigor, it's sensible to give yourself a full sprint cycle at a minimum.

The flipside to this maxim is, *don't plan a collaboration that is longer than 12 sprints.* That is, even if you need longer than three months to actually develop a solution, or are working in a context that requires much longer timeframes, it's generally good to push the team to make one pass through the entire cycle in three months. This means you're socializing ideas and testing them with some frequency to avoid team insularity from taking you too far off course without feedback. I've worked on complicated hardware products where it took 16+ weeks and a quarter-million dollars to prototype the full system, but we would still look to prototype and test pieces or low-fidelity solutions more quickly to mitigate risk and learn about our guesses.

So the basic range you should plan in is 1–12 one-week sprints. But that's a lot of variation. How can you narrow this down? The sidebar "How Long Do I Need?" shows you specifically how to lead a team through estimating how long the entire effort might take, and what assumptions underlie that estimate. Again, it's worth reminding yourself and the team that this isn't about promising a deliverable, but about giving stakeholders some expectations about the complexity and approach the team thinks is best.

Tools to Help Plan Your Collaboration: How Long Do I Need?

If the team has prior experience, you likely already know the speed at which they work. If it's a new group, you can estimate how many ideas they can generate and test in a cycle. For example, if you have a team of four software engineers, a designer, a researcher, and a product manager, you might be able to assume that you could make four tries a week in paper or low-fidelity clickthroughs. If higher fidelity is needed, it may be that only one or two efforts can happen in a week.

The framework from Figure 5-5 helps you think through your approach as follows. If you have a simple problem with few stakeholders, you are likely doing work that is closer to co-creation or cooperation than true collaboration. Remember that cooperation describes the kind of groupwork where the order and contents of the work are well understood and you can better predict both how people should work and what the answer is likely to be. This describes basic work on, say, a new feature for a sprint where all of the details of how it will work are unknown, but the team can easily decide them and test them with users to refine it.

If you have a relatively simple problem, but not a lot of trust from stakeholders about the solutions, you should focus on creating data to earn that trust. Running a sprint or several sprints just focused on demonstrating how the team solves such problems, and how they are thoughtful about stakeholder interests, will help you instill confidence.

With more complex problems you should plan to spend a few cycles learning where the unknowns lie, and working closely with experts and stakeholders until it becomes simpler and can be executed on.

Being in the upper-right quadrant is tricky and will take time. You should budget a few cycles to try to reduce the unknowns you face into something better understood—by both the team and the stakeholders—to earn trust and build up the team's confidence. As you do, your secondary goal will be to use the trust you've built to gain some whitespace for the team to work under less (frequent) scrutiny.

Figure 5-10 shows an example of how you might plan out how long you need based on complexity.

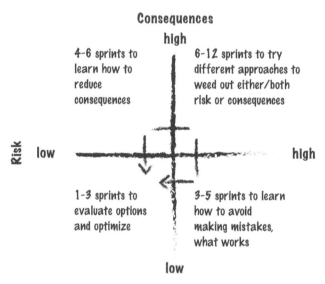

Consequences

high

4-6 sprints to learn how to reduce consequences

6-12 sprints to try different approaches to weed out either/both risk or consequences

Risk   low   high

1-3 sprints to evaluate options and optimize

3-5 sprints to learn how to avoid making mistakes, what works

low

Figure 5-10. Example timeframes for efforts of differing complexity

Your team's speed and the specifics of your situation may change the number of cycles you need. What's important is that you weigh the chances of making mistakes (risk) against what might happen if you do (consequences).

Share Plans to Set Expectations

Once you've created a plan, be sure to make it visible not just to the team, but to outsiders as well. Consider plans as you would work output, something that falls under the RACI roles you've hopefully established. Plans should be socialized widely—again, not as a promise, but as a guess about how the work will unfold.

This helps everyone have a sense of what to expect, and where the group is headed. For those who aren't dedicated full-time to the effort, it's especially useful to remind them where the team has been and where it's going.

Keeping track of your progress as you go doesn't just help you set expectations with stakeholders, it keeps the team focused. It can be easy to forget things you've learned, or take assumptions for granted if they aren't made explicit and visible. The sidebar "Keeping Track of Progress" offers tools for tracking and communicating your efforts.

Tools to Help Plan Your Collaboration: Keeping Track of Progress

Once you've planned out the work, it's important to keep track of the team's progress; otherwise, it's easy for the team to lose sight of what's happened and get lost in the current situation. It helps both team morale and communication with stakeholders when you can show how far you've come. You can use the template in Table 5-1 to track what work has been done, and what has been learned each time.

Table 5-1. A template for creating plans for your team and sharing with others

Objective(s):	# of experiments:	Key insights:
	Experiments per sprint:	Assumptions changed/confirmed:
	Assumptions tested:	KPIs/KFIs:

The biggest thing to remember when creating this plan is that you are managing expectations within the team about being intentional in their explorations and critiques with each other. You're also setting up external sessions to review the story of how the team is progressing. This worksheet can be your map of what you've tried and what you've shared, and will help keep continuity within the team.

Troubleshooting Planning

Issues that come up when you're making a plan for your team can involve external pressures, such as imposed deadlines, or internal pressures from the team itself. This section offers some suggestions for working through these problems.

WORKING AGAINST A FIXED DEADLINE

It's not always possible to predict how long it will take a team to tackle a complex problem with a lot of unknowns, and there will be times when a critical deadline must be met. In this situation, I've seen teams try to argue against the deadline and ask for more time, and never seen it work. Or, teams agree to a deadline with unrealistic expectations, only to miss it and suffer the consequences. In the situation where there is a key date that must be met, but not enough information to know how to get there, you run the risk of putting the group in jeopardy if you don't work to get more clarity.

So what can I do?

Define partial success

> To avoid having the collaboration get crushed under the weight of unreasonable expectations, focus instead on how you can get part of the way there, expressed in business terms, not features. If "sign up 2,000 paying customers" is what keeps the company afloat in three months, think about what you can do to get some of those financial results, rather than listing partial capabilities. In *Lean UX* (O'Reilly), Jeff Gothelf and Josh Seiden do a great job of laying out how to think outside the box to get results without overly committing to work that won't pay the full dividend in time.

Define the worst-case scenario

> It can be hard to be the person who speaks the truth about an ugly outcome. Early in my career, I faced extreme pressure to "be flexible" and agree to a client's demands even though they put their business at great risk. When the inevitable blow-up happened, it wasn't just unpleasant—several of my clients lost their jobs and the company eventually folded. The bad outcome that most of my team were focused on was displeasing the client, when in fact the worst case was so much worse than that. If you feel you've been given an impossible mandate, you owe it to yourself and others to make sure everyone understands what happens if (even though you know it's a "when") the team's efforts aren't totally successful.

Delay the "work" in favor of "workarounds"

While it might not be the most efficient way to get work done, if there really is a critical deadline, it may be better to develop a Band-Aid solution first. You will need to buy time later to create a real solution, but that will be easier to argue for when you've already met key requirements.

TEAMS RESIST PLANNING

There are times when teams will resist making and committing to a plan, especially if there are many unanswered questions. There can be a fear that by creating a plan they will be held to it no matter what happens. Things almost never go according to a plan, but the process of thinking through how you will all work together is still useful. If you can't all agree on how to approach the work, and set up points in time that others can expect to see progress, you will likely not get very far together.

Plans are also useful to keep stakeholders informed of progress and where you are in the cycle. They need to know if they are making decisions, exploring ideas, or defining problems to be able to contribute effectively.

So what can I do?

You Are Here

It isn't enough to have a timeline of the effort listing past meetings and future milestones to remind people of where the team is. You need to be clear about whether the group is open to exploring alternatives and gathering substantial input, or whether you're showing the output of a process simply to keep people updated. Don't try to mix those two modalities, no matter how tempting it may be. Telling people you want their input on possibilities, only to show them proposed solutions to be critiqued, is guaranteed to frustrate everyone. If you have a critical stakeholder who missed the "offer solutions" timeframe, consider making a special "traveling salesman" stop beforehand to get their input, and be clear that it isn't likely to be reflected immediately when they attend a session to update stakeholders on progress.

Frame it as a guess

I often coach teams to think about planning as fortune-telling, not a commitment. You can help alleviate fear of overpromising by asking the team to *guess* what could happen, and framing your plans with the right level of uncertainty when sharing with stakeholders. It is useful to consistently explain and show that plans are updated and changed as situations change so that people understand that the plan isn't a contract.

Conclusion

Structure is needed to keep teams from devolving or losing focus, especially when facing complex challenges. By understanding how ideas develop and setting up cycles of effort that are timeboxed and iterative, you can help teams de-risk situations and learn to reduce or avoid negative consequences that come from their solutions. The structure you create isn't meant to govern exactly what teams do or function as a monolithic order, but rather to help the core team and their stakeholders be explicit about where they are in their efforts and manage expectations. Plans should be made visible and revisited periodically to see what's changed and whether the effort needs a different approach.

Key Takeaways

- Collaborations can't succeed if they are free-for-all discussions without structure. People's personalities will lead to some dominating the work, or to teams getting lost between defining problems, solving them, and learning how well their solutions work.

- Creating a plan to help teams move through the cycle of exploration and learning helps mitigate risk.

- Plans don't have to be monolithic Gantt charts, but can be structured timeboxes that repeat as the team learns more and progresses.

- It's better to "guesstimate" how long the team needs and share those guesses to set expectations both within the team and with interested stakeholders.

6

Set Clear and Urgent Objectives

Almost all of the experts I spoke with brought up how crucial it is to understand the problem space and define the desired outcomes of a collaborative effort (see Figure 6-1); failure to do this well means your collaboration faces challenges right from the very start. With many people in the mix, it becomes very easy to get the group pulled in many directions. If you don't identify a clear objective, egos and competition are likely to take over, rather than enabling the group to pull together. In this chapter, we will look at what makes objectives useful, and how to create clear goals that unify efforts.

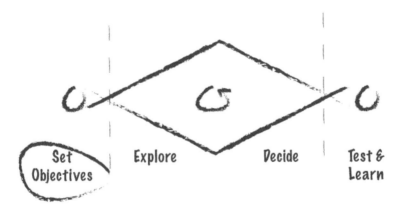

Figure 6-1. Setting (or resetting) objectives should happen at the start of every cycle the team goes through

"Shared context and goals are *the* most important thing that makes a team successful," says Michael Sippey, Head of Product at Medium. "I keep learning this truth. If the team isn't on the same page, they can't work well together." He believes his role as a leader is to create and maintain this focus for the group, and it's a task he takes seriously. "In the past, maybe I was clear on the objective, the context, but I didn't spend enough time and energy making sure everyone else was. When that happens the team feels whipsawed," and decisions start being made to protect individual interests instead of serving the desired outcomes.

It's not enough to simply state objectives. To be useful, objectives need to have a sense of urgency to them, and they need to be derived from a compelling vision.

Developing Good Objectives

There are many books and resources that describe the process of setting *objectives and key results*, or *OKRs*. This approach, which John Doerr brought to Google in 1999, has received a lot of positive attention as a method to create a shared mission and measurable results. Christina Wodtke's best-selling book, *Radical Focus* (Cucina Media), does a good job describing how OKRs work and how to use them. Like any framework, OKRs can yield good or bad results. What I find missing from much of the OKR discussion is guidance about what makes a *good* objective and how to create objectives well.

Good objectives need three things: to be descriptive, not prescriptive; to have a sense of urgency; and to be grounded in solving a problem or delivering a vision of the future that's compelling. When your objectives are well constructed, practices like OKRs can help make use of them. Leading a team through developing good objectives, rather than handing them down, is one way to get a shared understanding of what the group should focus on.

BE DESCRIPTIVE, NOT PRESCRIPTIVE

Developing direction that is *descriptive* of an end goal or outcome, rather than overly *prescriptive* of a solution, can be challenging. Military culture includes a concept known as the *commander's intent*, a succinct description of what constitutes success for a given mission. It contains the five Ws: who, what, when, where, and (most importantly) why the mission is being executed. Notice that the commander's intent does not specify *how* the mission will unfold. The reason for this is simple: a commander is situated far from the action on the ground, ignorant of the realities of terrain, weather, logistics, and more. Central command is responsible for driving large objectives that may be made up of interlocking missions, such as controlling a specific bit of territory by one group to defend another. Units on the ground often lack the larger context of other units, and so the chain of command leaves them a certain amount of freedom to act to achieve their objective, but not to invent their objective themselves.

I find this metaphor helpful when crafting direction for collaborative teams. It speaks to lines of authority that are useful, rather than micromanaging, while allowing teams to act with a degree of autonomy in a loosely coordinated fashion. Especially in large organizations, this interdependence is *critical* to being efficient with resources and allowing for the interchange of data and information, whether literally in terms of APIs and subsystems, or figuratively in terms of what's true across the organization. Establishing a commander's intent–like objective gives teams the freedom to decide how they will achieve the goal, but also allows for cross-coordination about the what, why, and when involved.

When working with leaders who tend to be overly prescriptive in their objective setting, invoking the five Ws of the commander's intent can help bring clarity, and has the advantage of making the team look like they're trying to make use of the chain of command rather than undermine it. If you think about some of the less helpful directives you've been given, they often consist almost entirely of overly detailed "hows" while being quite light in the other dimensions. Help leaders and teams alike to describe the objective better and get everyone off on the right foot.

HAVE A SENSE OF URGENCY

Good objectives will help teams understand what's at stake in the effort and provide a sense of urgency to keep it from devolving under pressure. One example of how a sense of urgency is helpful comes from John Rosenberg, an ER doctor serving patients in Oakland and Richmond, California. He supports a lower-income population that faces tough challenges daily, many of them life-threatening. Not only does he treat patients who are suffering the effects of a trauma or major illness, but he also sees those grappling with mental health issues, domestic violence, and more.

In this setting a doctor like Rosenberg is expected—and required—to work with many different kinds of people, from technicians to nurses to administrators, to handle a case. In some cases, say a problematic pregnancy that requires immediate intervention, he may have upward of 20 people directly involved in the care of the patient: NICU specialists, OB specialists, nurses, family members, and more.

When asked how collaboration happens in an environment with that many stakeholders, many of them experts in their field, with the clock ticking and someone's life on the line, he said, "It comes down to having clear roles and clear guidelines for what we choose to do." He describes his mental model of emergency medicine as a type of "algorithm," where the team looks at evidence and then considers a small number of possible actions in response. Rosenberg says what enables the team to work this way is the clear focus on the life of the patient above all else. The ER can be an intense setting with a lot of moving parts: "It's really chaos in there, when everything is happening. There so many people and things move so quickly, but we know that the patient is our main focus. When I am the primary doctor on the case, I need to make sure that no one loses sight of them," he says.

Most collaborations in business aren't literally a matter of life and death, but almost every objective in business seems urgent. Certainly pressure to "deliver" is omnipresent in business. But the drive to complete things quickly often masks the actual reasons why solving the problem is critical. Looking deeper at collaborations that struggled to engage a wider group, I often found that there were real things at stake, but the "brief" given to the team focused less on those critical *outcomes* and more on *outputs*. Teams must know what happens if they fail, or if they make poor decisions, to be properly motivated to overcome interpersonal dynamics and keep up their stamina for the duration. Consider that "failure" for many collaborations may mean that a siloed Band-Aid solution is created, or that the group loses steam or is consumed by conflict until it dissolves and people retreat back into their silos. It's helpful to think about what would happen if you did nothing as another way to understand what's at stake.

GROUND OBJECTIVES IN SOLVING REAL-WORLD PROBLEMS

We may often think we have a sense of urgency in our efforts because of that dreaded workplace reality: deadlines. While timeboxing and deadlines have their place, they alone aren't enough to create the radical clarity and alignment that Rosenberg sees in the ER. Sara Ortloff Khoury, head of UX for Google Hire, found herself facing great pressure when she joined a startup that, like many, had a general sense of the domain they wanted to serve but hadn't yet developed a clear focus on the product offering. The team had done enough investigation to know that the current tools used by recruiters, HR professionals, and hiring managers were overly complicated and disliked by many—a market ripe for disruption. Their competitive analysis was thorough and clearly pinpointed places for improvement. But, as Khoury began to realize, while knowing what you *aren't* doing might be helpful, it's hardly a rallying cry.

Khoury knew that the team needed a better objective, and her experience in the industry taught her a sure-fire way to find one: focus on the users who will be served by the collaboration, rather than on the competition. She knew that understanding people who do hiring would help the startup focus on alleviating those users' frustrations, and that her team needed to feel that frustration firsthand to have a sense of urgency about *something* other than "ship fast and frequently."

Defining objectives as the solving of specific problems for specific users is one of the best ways to create alignment and purpose in a team. User-centered design and "talking to users" are a core part of many teams, especially those that include experienced design- and UX-focused members. But in many of the collaborations I have seen and studied, that work can happen off to the side or be done by specialists, and isn't always taken to heart by the team. Khoury decided to change that and enlist her team to identify more deeply with their users.

At the same time, the startup was being acquired by Google, which brought in a whole new set of stakeholders and opinions that needed alignment. Clearly, Khoury wasn't going to bring dozens of people into primary research with potential customers, but as it turned out, she didn't need to. When the team came back together to look at what they had learned, they found they had a clear, focused objective that had been there all along: people didn't want more features or a better version of the tools they had; users were frustrated by systems that had very rigid flows and business process rules to support work that was often personal and highly varied. The team saw how tools meant to help a process had in fact slowed things down as users added head count and workarounds to support the tools, instead of being supported by them. The problem wasn't with the tools themselves, but rather the gaps and walls between them.

Getting a team to understand what's at stake can be challenging when specific problems or opportunity costs aren't clear or haven't been quantified. Grounding your work in solving problems for people and understanding the stakes (as exhibited by the "pain" users experience) is a better way to make objectives real than meeting specific metrics or leading indicators.

Approaches and Techniques for Creating Objectives

DERIVE OBJECTIVES FROM A PROBLEM

While the commander's intent is a useful construct to think about setting direction, we can be more specific about what exactly an objective that isn't overly prescriptive looks like. Figure 6-2 shows a framework I use to create objectives. You can use this to create your own objectives and set a vision from scratch, or to back people up from solutions to divine more helpful objectives.

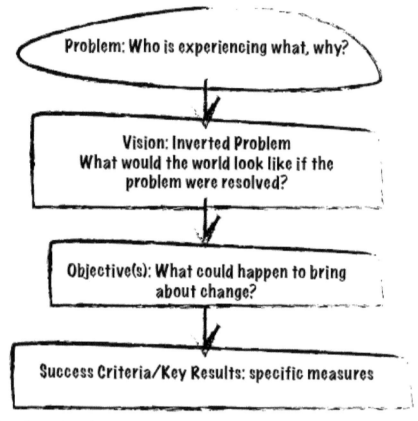

Figure 6-2. Deriving objectives from the problems you are looking to solve and the vision you want to bring about

First, ground your team in a problem (see the sidebar "Defining the Problem" for tips). That's a good way to ensure that the work holds value. In the previous section you saw how understanding the customer you're serving helps you create a compelling vision of the future to aim for. (That said, there are times when you're not so much facing a clear problem as trying to avoid opportunity costs.)

Tools to Create Clear Goals and Objectives: Defining the Problem

Even if you've been handed a problem that seems clear and is widely understood, it's worth taking the team through an exercise to dig into *why* the problem is occurring and how you know that.

1. Start with what you've been given. Likely, there's already an articulation of what's wrong. Capture the given situation and then refine it by asking yourselves a few key questions:

   - Who is being affected? How are they experiencing negative consequences?
   - What is the impact of the problem? What is it "costing" the company and those affected? This doesn't necessarily have to be described as financial impact, but it needs to imply the value of actually fixing the problem.
   - When/how often is the problem happening?

2. Identify the causes.

   - Why is the problem occurring? You may not know, but you can investigate or make some guesses that you can test.
   - What trends or changes are occurring that might cause a problem in the future?

The framework shown in Figure 6-3 can help you create objectives in a structured way. You can capture your problem(s) in a crisp statement using the statement template.

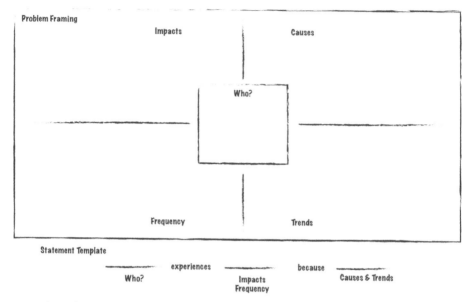

Figure 6-3. Frame problems by looking at the factors that surround them

TURN PROBLEM STATEMENTS INTO OBJECTIVES

Once you have a clear understanding of what problem you're solving, you can flip it around to create a vision statement. What would it look like if that problem were solved? What would be enabled? What would be avoided?

These two pieces are helpful to express clearly because the team can turn back to them when they're stuck or if something they tried doesn't work. The problem and vision statement don't say what the solution is, but they describe the outcomes that are needed.

Next, frame useful objectives by having a clear sense of who benefits from the objective, what that benefit is, and what root causes have been addressed. If possible, set a goal for when the problem will be solved.

The template I use is shown in Figure 6-4.

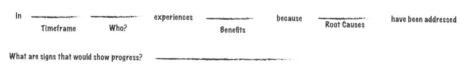

Figure 6-4. A template for stating objectives

Here are some examples of objectives that use this format:

By 2020, Californians will impact climate change by transitioning to fully renewable, carbon-free energy sources.

Customers who are financial novices will have increased savings and greater confidence in their ability to save money when they see suggestions for less expensive products and services that they regularly buy.

Employees who commute more than 20 minutes each way to work will be more productive when they can choose to work remotely, or use transportation that allows them to work while commuting.

Finally, success criteria are also important to state clearly. The simplest way to think of success criteria or key results is to ask, what indicators would tell us that the problem is solved or getting better? These can be very quantifiable or qualitative, depending on what you can actually measure. Don't throw away leading indicators that you think would be good success criteria, even if you can't measure them. With time and persistence, you may find a way to get that data, and then you can replace criteria that aren't good predictors but are easy to measure.

REFINE OBJECTIVES TO BE MORE USEFUL

In his book *The Logic of Failure* (Basic Books), Dietrich Dörner shows how goals can be formulated in useful and productive ways. He lays out key characteristics of goals, and their strengths and weaknesses, along some key axes:

Positive or negative
Goals can be statements of what you are trying to achieve, or conversely, what you want to avoid. It's better to specify goals positively, however, because they will be more specific (see the next point) and will serve the team as a more productive starting point.

General or specific
General goals are often where we start out—stating a view of what we'd like to see, but without a lot of details. Being as specific as possible without being overly prescriptive helps teams focus their energy and makes outcomes more measurable. Where possible, create specific statements of the objective, even if that specificity evolves over time as you better learn what will support the objective.

Singular or multiple

Some goals stand on their own, with a single outcome being chased. But very often, we are dealing with complex systems where one objective relates to another, and not always in a straightforward way. Look to simplify or prioritize complex goals where possible, but avoid oversimplifying goals in pursuit of clarity.

Implicit or explicit

One of the biggest traps teams fall into is having implicit goals that go unstated, only to arise as a key factor once they begin testing their solutions. Where possible, strive to clearly state goals, even if they seem obvious or are assumed to be shared.

These refinement techniques can be applied to objectives that you have developed or to objectives that you have been given as a starting point. For example, imagine you are asked to create a system that:

- Helps charitable organizations grow their audience and raise funds from more people

- Is easy to use

- Is less expensive than currently available tools

The first goal seems clear enough; it's positively framed and mostly singular. But it's a bit general, and could benefit from some details about how much more money and people we are talking about. There's also an implicit idea that all charitable organizations are actually seeking to reach more people, rather than raising more funds from a smaller base. Those two things are linked objectives here, but ones that we might want to learn more about as we go.

The second goal more obviously needs help. "Easy to use" is a goal teams are given often. We acknowledge that making things that are easy to use will help us sell them and gain loyalty from customers, but can we do better here? What about "Requires no training"? That's nice and simple, though it is negatively framed. It might be better to add, "Self-guided exploration is enough for people to use successfully." That's clunky, so keeping the headline of "Needs no training" may be preferable, but you can use the more specific, positive expression when you're evaluating whether your solutions actually need this objective.

The last objective is general, but it does have some comparison points to existing tools. It's not very useful for a team getting started, however. This might be an objective to keep an eye on to understand what drives costs and then state that more clearly, as in "Requires only X customer service agents per Y customers."

See the sidebar "Refining Objective(s)" for further advice on structuring your objectives to be more useful.

Tools to Create Clear Goals and Objectives: Refining Objective(s)

Once you've got a clear statement of the problem and the objective(s), go through and refine them along the axes that Dörner's research identifies. The framework in Figure 6-5 can help structure discussions about objectives to make them even sharper.

- **Positive or negative.** If you have an objective that is expressed as something to avoid, try to frame the objective positively instead. Having negative objectives or a sense of what to avoid can be useful, but try as well as you can to pair negative goals with positive ones. Can you frame the objective as something to be created, with the negative objective as a limitation or threshold to keep in mind? For example: Create new sales channel while not reducing the existing channel more than X%.

- **General or specific.** Rephrase general statements about the outcome, like "improve the experience," in more specific terms. This is a good place to bring the success criteria you've identified into the picture and see how specific you can make them. You might make an "easy to use" ordering system objective more specific by describing things like responsiveness, time to learn the system, how well users understand the status of their order, and so on.

- **Singular or multiple.** If you (likely) have some interrelated goals and success criteria to address, see if you can prioritize or rank them. You may also need to model how multiple goals relate. For example, if you want to introduce new capabilities to the market, you may also need to pay attention to decreasing usage of existing offerings and impacting revenue adversely.

- **Implicit or explicit.** Look for implicit goals by asking what is being taken for granted. List out things in the environment or system that would be problematic if they didn't exist, and make sure you acknowledge them as explicit parts of the solution.

- **Additional audiences.** See if there are other users or interested parties that weren't originally identified that need to be taken into consideration.

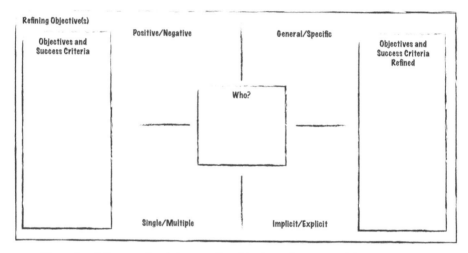

Figure 6-5. A framework to help you refine objectives to be more useful and specific

Learning to refine and express objectively more clearly is a key part of mastering collaboration. This can and should happen up front, as you are getting started, but as we've seen, many times we need to revisit our goals as we work to incorporate what we've learned. It's also common that we don't see our implicitly assumed objectives until we get into the work and start to see things we took for granted at the outset. Make time not just to set clear objectives, but also to revisit and refine them as you go.

KEEP TRACK OF KNOWLEDGE AND ASSUMPTIONS

Especially at the beginning of an effort, setting objectives may require the group to make some assumptions about the problem, its causes, and what a vision of success would look like. This can feel uncomfortable for some who fear making a misstep. Others are all too happy to make assumptions and never look back. Keeping track of the assumptions you make and supporting them with data and facts as you go is critical (see the sidebar "Expressing Assumptions" for more on this topic). Assumptions are often made implicitly and left unstated, which can lead the group astray. When assumptions are met with evidence to the contrary, they are hard to change if they aren't made explicit. Instead, the group can tend to devolve into debate about the evidence that is more visible. It's a good idea to always pair stated goals and objectives with key assumptions. If we revisit the earlier example about helping charitable organizations, some key assumptions are being made that people understand the value of giving to charity, and that we can acquire customers by converting them from existing services easily—both things that could easily be tested to see how they hold up.

Tools to Create Clear Goals and Objectives: Expressing Assumptions

Having good raw material about your problem is key, but it can also be helpful to express the problem in a consistent way so the different components are transparent to others. Refer back to the simple template in Figure 6-3 for stating problems clearly.

The next step is to analyze *how* you know what the problem is and what causes it. There's nothing wrong with making guesses or hypotheses about what's happening, as long as you keep track of them. Lead the team through a discussion about what information is based on evidence, and what is anecdotal or assumed. This allows you to refine how you express your problem and keep assumptions top of mind (see Figure 6-6).

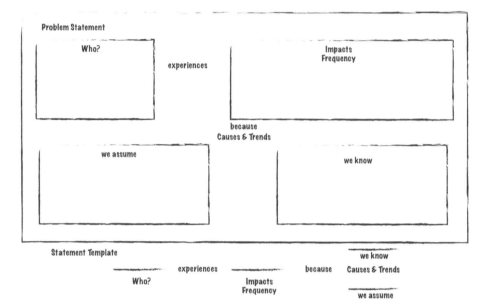

Figure 6-6. Analyzing how you know what the problem is and what causes it

Now that you understand the problem and have expressed it clearly, you can invert it to create statements about what you want to achieve to solve it.

1. Define the objective(s).

   — What is the inverse of the impacts you've identified? What would the world look like if the problem were solved? What benefits will people derive from the end result?

   — Which of the causes you've identified can the team work to stop, slow, or improve?

2. Identify success criteria.

   — What are some signs of success that you would expect to see if we achieved the objective? (See Figure 6-7.)

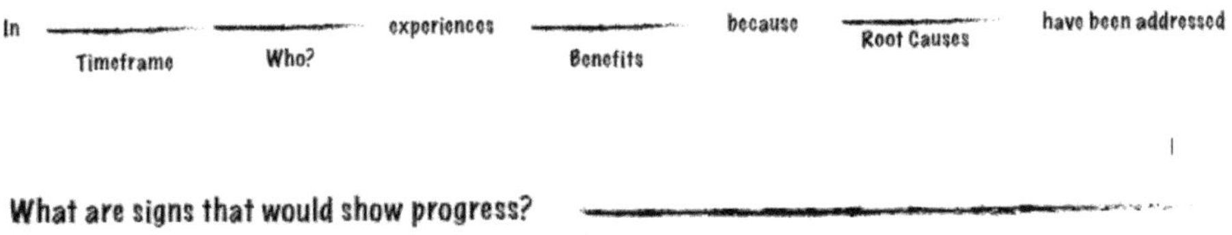

In ——————— ——————— experiences ——————— because ——————— have been addressed

Timeframe   Who?   Benefits   Root Causes

What are signs that would show progress? ————————————————————————

Figure 6-7. A template for including signs of progress

USE THE "WHITEPAPER APPROACH"

Under Jeff Bezos's guidance, teams at Amazon take a very thorough approach to capturing and sharing objectives. For major initiatives, especially those with a lot of context, teams produce a short, three- to five-page *whitepaper* laying out the challenge and the objective for their work and use that to plan and review different workstreams. This approach is also used by Michael Sippey, Head of Product at Medium, to help himself as leader keep track of many interrelated efforts at a macro level. The whitepapers his teams use are simple arguments about what work the team thinks is necessary, and why. The whitepapers also describe a theory about what tactical moves the team can make to achieve their goal. While writing a short essay may seem like a lot of work, this technique is embraced in many companies because it forces the team to fully think through their argument, rather than writing a few bullet points.

One benefit Sippey calls out is how it changes the dynamic in the room so it's more conducive to good critique than using slides would be: "Slides suck for actually helping people comprehend an argument, because the only person who has the context is the presenter. It always feels like trying to ask a question results in, 'Wait for the next slide, I'll get to that,'" making it hard to put the full picture together. He also appreciates the use of time together more. "Being together [in that way] reminds you of the camaraderie in the team; it makes people act better, and forces me to be more thoughtful," he says. This isn't to say there isn't dissent, but it will tend to be "the thing about the thing," rather than personal attacks. If he does have particularly harsh feedback for a team or an individual, he tends to communicate privately to avoid "trashing anyone in public." This, in turn, bolsters the quality of critique without sacrificing rigorous debate.

At Google, many product teams use the whitepaper approach to guide executive reviews of work being planned. Given the scope of what the org covers—

billions of users, tens of thousands of employees—they need a way to build a shared understanding of priorities, and support executives in making critical decisions or approvals. Teams are charged with developing whitepapers about who they served, what key insights they've discovered about the market, and what types of features should be developed to best meet the demands on their product.

Those I spoke with had many different ways of creating whitepapers, such as empowering a single author that asks for input on drafts or having a team fully co-create the paper from notes on a whiteboard through to a finished draft. For teams who don't have some stability and experience around the work they are doing, co-creation may be a great way to build that. For teams that have fewer unknowns about the future of their product, it might be fine to empower a single author who gets reviewed.

If the whitepaper approach is one you want to try or one you are already doing, consider shifting the dissemination and reading of the whitepaper ahead of the meeting time you have set up. Especially for those with learning disabilities, those first 10 minutes of silent reading may be disquieting and unproductive. Dyslexics are quite capable of reading many pages of material, but they may prefer to do it through their ears by using text to speech, or to have their own time and space to process, rather than reading in public. This can also be helpful for nonnative speakers of the dominant language who, having to rely solely on a presenter or a short, fixed time to read, could be at a disadvantage.

It is also a good idea to make sure that the request to write a whitepaper is framed as an exercise that serves the team—and it should come from those closest to the problem, not a lone product manager laying out their view or seeing it as a long-form status report. When teams write whitepapers for executives, rather than to get clarity for themselves, the quality of the argument may not be as high. Besides, a thesis generated by and for the team will naturally satisfy executives too.

There's nothing wrong with stating objectives in a short format versus the whitepaper approach. What's important is to develop clear objectives and know how to measure them. How you choose to socialize them and help others internalize them can vary.

Keep Objectives Visible, and Revisit Them Periodically

Objectives need to be actively maintained, and can't be taken for granted after you've learned something new. "You have to actively question your starting point," Michael Sippey says, "because the context changes, and too often we leave that unsaid." He uses the stated objectives and assumptions as a touchstone, and takes time to make sure they are shared and understood by everyone who wants to participate.

Keep objectives visible, perhaps posted in the working space, and refer back to them at the start and end of sessions working together. As the group internalizes their objective, they can use it to provide focus and urgency when the going gets tough, or to inspire ideas and critique rather than always starting from a blank slate. Over time, objectives can shift, especially as assumptions are tested and the team learns more. Take time at the beginning of every cycle of exploration to use what you've learned to refine the team's direction. And be sure to always take stakeholders, and any others who aren't fully immersed in the effort, through the evolving objectives to ground them and provide the needed context for decisions and feedback.

When Learning Is the Objective

What about when there isn't an actual urgent problem facing the team? Obviously not every engagement contains the threat of serious consequences if it goes wrong. Often these situations are really about helping a group learn a new way to operate, something that is very en vogue with the push toward "digital transformation" in business. Companies looking to create a less hierarchical, order-taking culture often see collaboration as a way to bring about the change they want. And they aren't wrong. However, setting teams up to collaborate on such a challenge invites their first efforts to seem like yet another annoying bit of change management; no one wants to feel they are the ones rearranging deck chairs on the *Titanic*.

For those teams who need to develop new muscles, there's nothing wrong with doing the work for the sake of learning. You just need to be very explicit about it. Collaborating when learning to collaborate is the goal just means that there are some fundamental shifts in how you frame the work and set up the team:

- Short challenges with a known "answer"
- Emphasis on helping everyone get to the answer together
- Showing your work

When I observed kids learning collaboration in the classroom, that was certainly the case. In Ms. Susan's fourth-grade classroom in the Bay Area, kids often work in groups to solve puzzles and teach each other different ways to get there. These efforts tend to be more of a learning or training opportunity, which also holds great value, than true collaboration. But putting teams and students in this situation means that leaders need to be clear that the outcome is to learn, not necessarily to produce.

Because he needs his teams to work as flawlessly as possible under tough conditions in the ER, Dr. Rosenberg says working in a more "academic" setting to practice for the real thing has incredible value. "We run drills for some of the most complicated situations we may see," he says, "that way we can make sure everyone understands their role in how decisions will get made, as well as addressing some very basic information needs." This might mean a nurse learning how to power up an infrequently used piece of equipment, or finding the right collection of phone numbers to call when situations go from bad to worse.

Having learning as an objective can be very useful; just make sure that the team is clear that the effort isn't about tackling an immediate problem, but about working on a longer-term objective. In the case of ER drills, the result isn't the saving of a life in that moment, but making sure that the team is ready when that moment comes.

Troubleshooting Objective Setting

Setting objectives is a critical step, but one that can be tricky to get right. This section gives suggestions for overcoming common problems teams run into.

OVERLY PRESCRIPTIVE DIRECTION

It's very common that when faced with a question, people offer specific solutions versus general criteria about what a good solution looks like. For teams who need to be able to explore different possibilities and gather data about what works from a realistic trial, this can be challenging—especially when the solution is given by a senior leader or expert whose opinion is respected, or whose authority is intimidating. More often than not, when the CEO tells you their solution to a challenge, they are offering an example meant to inspire investigation, not an order. I've watched teams jump through hoops to implement a leader's idea, only to be surprised to hear them say, "I didn't mean it literally!"

The tendency to speak in terms of tangible solutions also results in a run-off between different guesses about what will work, even if they aren't easily comparable. This can turn discussion into a popularity contest between ideas or those who offer them.

So what can I do?

Add it to the list
> Because specific solutions are often not meant to be taken as gospel, it's useful to write them down on a list and save them for later. It's not useful to argue the merits of an idea that hasn't been thought through completely. Instead, keep track of it and use it for inspiration. Having a record of what others have offered is also useful when presenting work for them to review later. You can refer back to their specifics, and then show how the idea has evolved or pivoted based on what the team has learned.

Back it up
> Being able to take someone's specific solution and back up to the general characteristics it implies is a skill worth mastering. This is easier if the group has some general success criteria identified and can relate the idea to them. You can ask "Why is that idea good?" to get the person to think and talk about the motivations for their solution, minus specifics. By backing the person up to articulate and understand the goals behind their solution, you help everyone get clarity about where the group should be headed.

CONSEQUENCES NOT CLEAR

When the team doesn't know what's at stake, the interpersonal dynamics can turn into conflicts when things get challenging. If the group doesn't have the equivalent of a patient whose life is in danger, fear of failure can make them turn on each other.

So what can I do?

Create worst-case scenarios
> It can actually be fun to spend a bit of time dreaming up situations gone wrong. Asking the group to think about possible unintended consequences of their work isn't a strictly analytical process, and takes some creative thinking. This can also be a way to warm up for developing solutions, as people begin thinking about factors that are not obvious.

Identify potential bad actors

> While understanding your users or target audience for solutions is important, it's also worth thinking about those who might abuse the system. Have the group develop profiles for bad actors to think through what might motivate them to act out. It's also useful to test ideas for ways they can be subverted by asking, "What if our bad actor used this?" so you can defend against them.

Look for instructive examples of comparable failures

> There is a lot to learn from others' mistakes. Ask the team to research embarrassing or dangerous situations that competitors or those with comparable problems have experienced, and see if you might be facing a similar vulnerability.

CONSTANT QUESTIONING OF OBJECTIVES

In some groups friction arises that keeps them at square one, continually debating assumptions rather than developing hypotheses that can be tested to turn unknowns or guesses into something concrete. At its root, this behavior stems from fear—fear of being wrong and facing the consequences of failure. At times, this can also happen when the group lacks experience with developing hypotheses and experimentation.

So what can I do?

Co-create and refine objectives together

> Don't simply take what you've been handed as a starting point and run with it. Spend a few hours or days working through objectives to make sure they are understood, and to air out concerns the team has.

Revisit objectives periodically

> If you establish a practice of revisiting objectives often, you also help signal to the team that objectives can and will evolve, and make room for questioning "givens" that may prove to be flexible over time.

JUKING THE STATS

The epic television drama *The Wire*, about crime and life in Baltimore, has several great set pieces about "juking the stats," where cops focus on getting the numbers right, by any means necessary. "You make robberies into larcenies," says one of the characters. "You juke the stats, and majors become colonels."

Watch out for teams that chase the numbers but lose sight of what those metrics were really supposed to indicate.

When I led product management and development at GreatSchools, a Yelp-like website with ratings and reviews for every school in the US, we worked hard to get schools to supply more information about themselves on the site and engage with their families to strengthen the school-home connection. Our target of having a certain percent of schools claim their profile online was ambitious, and reaching schools difficult. The team hired several people to scrape the web for information to display on the site. While it increased the data we had, it failed to reach the real goal—connecting schools and parents.

So what can I do?

Be descriptive

Use the previous exercises to develop a clear description of what you are looking to achieve, avoiding general goals, and simplifying and modeling objectives that are complex and interrelated. Keep your team focused on the objective, not simply the leading indicators you've established, so that they themselves can spot when something meets the key performance indicators (KPIs) but doesn't deliver the outcome.

Manage a portfolio of measures

Rather than trying to nail one, or even all, of your OKRs, think of them as a portfolio of early indicators that should tell you *directionally* if you are doing the right thing. Be sure to underscore that OKRs aren't grades, and making them won't get anyone promoted the way "SMART" performance goals may have worked in the past.

Conclusion

Setting objectives is a critical skill to master to set direction for the team. It's worth spending time as a team and with stakeholders to develop and express objectives that are descriptive, have a clear sense of urgency, and tie to a vision of the future and solving a real-world problem. Revisiting objectives frequently and refining them as you learn more should be a standard part of your practice.

Key Takeaways

- Every effort should have clear objectives to guide the work and fight against tendencies to get distracted by different problems or solutions.

- Good objectives are derived from the problem you want to solve, and aren't overly prescriptive of what solutions the team should implement. Teams need to know what's at stake in their efforts, so create objectives with a sense of urgency to them.

- Objectives shouldn't just be taken as a given, but refined to be specific and useful to avoid having an ill-defined target that doesn't help the team evaluate different ideas.

- A team's objective may be simply to learn how to work together, rather than solve a problem with no known solution, but that should be made clear.

- Whatever the team's objective is, make sure it is transparently shared within the team and with stakeholders to avoid clashes when expectations don't match up.

Exploring Solutions

Collaboration is necessary when teams are seeking solutions that aren't obvious or facing unknowns that carry risks. Being able to bring a group together in the right environment and give them a good start helps them be productive. It's also important, however, to get them out of their comfort zone so they can seek new answers, and to share those ideas early and often to learn and refine them. In this part we look at ways you can support the exploration of ideas more widely and channel critiques and feedback constructively.

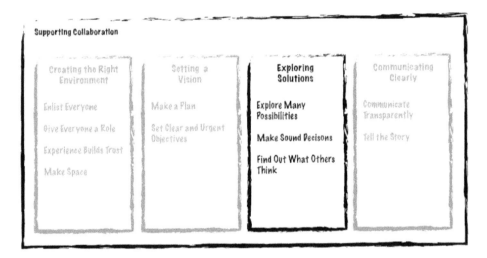

Supporting Collaboration

Creating the Right Environment	Setting a Vision	Exploring Solutions	Communicating Clearly
Enlist Everyone	Make a Plan	Explore Many Possibilities	Communicate Transparently
Give Everyone a Role	Set Clear and Urgent Objectives	Make Sound Decisons	Tell the Story
Experience Builds Trust		Find Out What Others Think	
Make Space			

7

Explore Many Possibilities

In this chapter we'll look at ways you can harness the power of your team to generate diverse—even wildly impractical—ideas that help lead to innovative solutions. What's key here is to be deliberate about thinking in an open-ended way, getting rid of constraints and generating ideas separately from evaluating them and making them more practical. This generally happens every cycle, after objectives have been set or revisited (Figure 7-1).

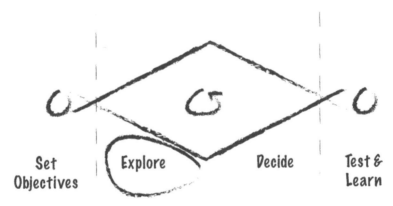

Figure 7-1. *Exploring ideas and deciding which to pursue should happen each cycle, or even multiple times in a cycle*

During this stage, we must be intentional about driving divergent thinking, because it doesn't happen naturally. As we build up our expertise and reputation for deeply understanding a domain, what makes it work, and what makes it break, we can tend to shut off being expansive in our thinking. This can lead to blind spots and limitations when we want to innovate. You've probably witnessed brainstorm meetings where most of the ideas offered are retreads of things already being done, or pet ideas pushed by a coalition convinced they've won the guess-a-thon. Idea generation can also be stifled by those who can't get past constraints and shoot down new ways of thinking.

Teams also need help productively critiquing ideas as a group to understand what's working, and to refine those they want to take to a wider audience. Deciding what ideas to prototype or test can fall prey to the tendency to select safe ideas or those that are favored by more senior people or experts. Being able to analyze different ideas, especially those that aren't ruled by constraints, to make them stronger and more practical is a skill you can develop and use to help others. Because this process can be challenging and introduce a lot of conflict, it's a good idea to do at least some of it in a safe space with the core team first. You can bring in others once the group has some confidence in their ability to attack the problem and can speak clearly about constraints and what makes ideas good. Remember our framework for understanding different types of contributors from Chapter 2 (Figure 7-2).

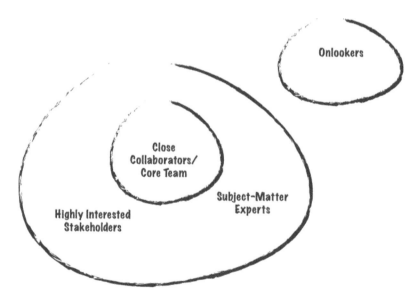

Figure 7-2. Understanding different types of contributors to a collaboration

If you can help teams generate new ideas with those outside the group, you can arrive at some great solutions. At Pacific Gas and Electric, which serves Northern California and is the largest energy utility in the US, I worked with teams to develop digital tools to help workers build, maintain, and operate over 141,000 miles of electrical wires and over 40,000 miles of gas pipeline. Robert Bales of McKinsey worked hard to make sure that in collaboration workshops, we always included the field workers in the ideation, because they knew the details of how the system worked and what it took to support it. But they also turned out to be the most inventive thinkers on the team. Every session, these grizzled, seasoned engineers would tell us how they weren't "really into technology" and could "barely work this fancy phone."

In one session, an engineer was describing the challenges of searching for gas leaks underwater. In a moment of frustration, he blurted out, "I just wish I had a gas-sniffing dolphin!" to the merriment of his colleagues. But to the digital technology people in the room, this was a breakthrough, because they understood that fitting sensors onto an underwater drone was absolutely possible, and not nearly as complicated as some of the Rube Goldberg ideas that had been developed so far. It turns out that being naive about technology made the engineers better able to see through to solutions.

Sometimes, the biggest challenge we face is to imagine the unimaginable, but when we do, it often becomes more possible to conceive of as reality. And that reality can also be much simpler to achieve than the crazy idea that spawned the new way of thinking. In the case of gas-sniffing dolphins, it was the engineer's ability to articulate the ideal state machine to solve the problem, no matter how fantastical, that led the group to see a simple solution. Solving for or relaxing constraints once new ideas have been generated is often easier than it might seem initially.

Working Backward, Thinking Laterally

Alan Cooper, founder of the consultancy Cooper and father of Visual Basic, calls this approach "working backward." He has spoken frequently about how in business people typically try to take a linear, forward working approach, piling analysis upon analysis until they hopefully arrive at the right destination. The problem, he points out, is that this approach tends to not have any concept of what that destination is, at least not in a way that is helpful.

Instead, he argues that when we have a clear vision of where we want to go—an objective that is explicit and concrete—we can work backward from there, casting about for possibilities to see if they lead in that direction. And because this way of working isn't linear and analytical, it requires enabling some magical thinking among the team.

In his book *The Design of Business* (Harvard Business), Roger Martin talks about how typically companies are quite good at optimizing and streamlining processes that are well understood—working forward, in essence, toward efficiency (see the top of Figure 7-3). But most organizations struggle with "mysteries" where things aren't predictable or analyzable in the same way. When a company seeks a competitive advantage or an innovative approach to a problem, digging deeper into analysis isn't likely to bear fruit; it just gets them deeper in the same hole.

This push for data-driven optimization doesn't apply only to manufacturing or production processes, either. I once worked for a large electronics manufacturer to help develop a strategy for a mobile cloud offering that would not just compete with Apple and others industry leaders, but actually overtake them. The company culture was so strictly analytical, so "data-driven," that not a single idea could be raised that wasn't derived from data. In their minds, the process of innovation was an algorithm, like a perfectly executed Google query that would tell them exactly what steps to take. It was completely lost on them that even had I been able to deliver such an algorithm, there was nothing to stop their competitors from doing the same thing. And if data existed to tell us where a solution lay, it followed that competitors must have arrived at that solution before *in order to create that data*. In the end, the strategy we offered was so data-driven that just three months after we presented it, a new challenger in the marketplace delivered a product offering that was almost identical. If a solution is well understood, it's because it already exists, and so it may not need a collaborative effort to invent it but more of a cooperative effort to build it.

One way to stop analysis paralysis and help teams deal with "mysterious" challenges that don't have an obvious solution is *lateral thinking*, which is described by Edward de Bono in his 1970 book of the same name (Harper & Row). Lateral thinking is the practice of coming at a problem from different perspectives (some almost completely divorced from the problem) to arrive at innovative solutions that you might otherwise miss by simply analyzing your way toward a solution, building logical conclusion upon logical conclusion. I always think of Aristotle, the Greek mathematician who was struggling to find a way to calculate the volume of an irregularly shaped object. It was only when he put the problem to the side for a moment and got into the bath that he realized that an object's volume is equal to the amount of water it displaces when submerged. These kinds of "eureka!" moments are at the heart of lateral thinking techniques.

To enable lateral thinking, you need to break the typical analytical processes that people use to derive answers in a linear fashion (see the bottom of Figure 7-3). When people come at a problem sideways, they may generate ideas that aren't feasible but, like gas-sniffing dolphins, can be tweaked to be feasible. Don't worry too much in early stages about generating ideas that aren't feasible. The goal is to get to the moment where an ideal solution is expressed. This doesn't come naturally to most people, but there are techniques you can use to divert the team's thinking and distract them from analyses and constraints so they get creative and generate new solutions.

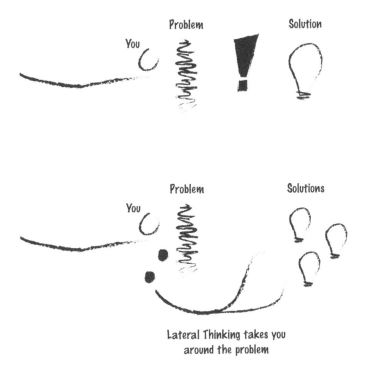

Lateral Thinking takes you
around the problem

Figure 7-3. Lateral thinking doesn't attack a problem head-on but instead tries to distract the mind and find ways around the problem

When you're working in this mode it's also good to push the team to generate many ideas, focusing on quantity over quality. If you can get enough ideas and cross-pollination among your diverse team members, you are more likely to have a breakthrough in the team's perspective that enables a shift toward new solutions.

Because lateral thinking isn't analytical or predictable, it works best when there's a vision to work backward from, as Cooper advises. The clear objectives and vision that you created in Chapter 6 should serve as the target for a team working in this nebulous space. This way of working will challenge many organizations, especially in the early days when the team doesn't yet have the answer and leaders get impatient without any obvious "progress." Help protect the team by not exposing them to outsiders at this time, or by doing it very carefully. It may take a few rounds of investigation with actual "users" of solutions to get data confirming that you are headed in a good direction, even if you aren't done. The best way to cope during this phase is to be strong throughout it and express how the team's work facilitates the vision of the future, not how they meet production deadlines.

Breaking out of the normal patterns of thinking and constraints will take some doing, but there are tangible techniques you can use to get your team there and make the most of their talents. What's key is that you make time and space for the team to explore new ideas safely, away from those who might want to fall back to known solutions or dwell on what can't be achieved rather than look for the new.

Throw Away Constraints, for a While

Being able to relax or work around constraints to get somewhere new is challenging. I once worked with a diverse team of talented engineers and leading physicians to develop a next-generation surgical robot capable of performing many different kinds of surgeries, unlike the models that were currently on the market, which could perform only a single therapy. The team spent years studying the problem and had invented incredible technology to solve different aspects, and it was time to put those together into a single system that could be used in the operating room. The question was how the doctors should control the machine. The physicians the team worked with were leaders in their fields and possessed amazing physical abilities to control manual tools; their dexterity and "touch" had gained them prestige and credibility in their field. But this system was designed to support those who *didn't* have that touch and could benefit from computer-aided support. To create a compelling demo for investors, the team needed a way to mimic the clunky manual controls that most doctors used, so they hit upon using a standard video game controller. Because video games were so far removed from the domain of surgery, no one seriously considered this to be a real answer to part of the problem. And, yet, once they had that demo, the entire company and their investors quickly realized that this approach was exactly what was needed—because video games, like surgical procedures, span a huge range of ways to move through space, from first-person shooters to third-person strategy games. All it took was for someone, under pressure, to decide to ignore the constraint of how surgeons typically worked, and choose a solution that supported many ways of controlling objects in space and apply it to a new domain.

WHAT ABOUT WHEN CONSTRAINTS ARE REAL?

When I coach teams to "throw away constraints," I often hear about how real those constraints are and how impossible or imprudent it is to ignore them. Of course the limitations on any problem are real, whether they are the laws of physics or legal regulations and requirements, but at the same time, if we don't open up our thinking beyond those limitations, the ideas and solutions we generate rarely end up in a new place. What's important to remember, and to help teams realize, is that you aren't actually getting rid of constraints but rather imagining they're not there, just for a short span of time, to see what you come up with in their absence. This is why the process is visualized as a diamond shape, where the group alternates between being expansive in their thinking and then bringing constraints back in to narrow down and refine their ideas.

Because many people are overly attached to constraints, taking them as givens that prescribe work and keep things realistic, teams need help with the "yeah-buts"—those who continually interrupt expansive thinking with "yeah, but what about X?" comments that shut down thinking. Sometimes you can actually change or work around constraints, as in the robotic surgery example where it was assumed that doctors needed the same sorts of controls they had in a nonrobotic world. Once you open the team up to what's possible, you'll find that many constraints turn out to be assumptions.

When constraints are real, such as regulatory rules, it's also possible that imagining a future with different constraints is actually more beneficial for everyone, and leads to arguments to change or evolve them. Once, a client was looking for ways to improve team collaboration and empower employees to be more autonomous. They had strict policies about expenses for employees at a certain level, requiring VP-level approval for everything from ordering lunches to obtaining supplies in an effort to control costs. As a result of the signoff requirement, rather than approach executives about small purchases, employees just didn't make them, instead "making do" even if it was challenging to end results. The team, working through different approaches to improve the working environment and drive decisions about key product features, continually ran into this constraint. They were good-natured about it, making jokes about the situation, but it was clear that the policy was literally and figuratively working against the very thing the company was trying to achieve. "If we aren't trusted to make decisions about spending $50 on food or supplies that we need, how do they expect us to make big decisions about what the company should do?" asked one participant. This frustration became the basis for a scenario where teams had a full P&L for each product that included a budget for their small expenses, removing the approval cycle and creating complete autonomy. They included a part of the story showing how executives were freed up from reviewing and approving the requests as well. When this idea was shared with executives, they were surprised that this had been such an issue. The team had assumed that the constraint was fixed, rather than something they could revisit with those who had created it. The rule change was a huge success across the board because, as it turns out, everyone resented seeking or being asked for approval on up to 50 purchases a week. The team achieved their objective by placing the constraint change in a constructive scenario that showed the overall benefits, rather than arguing on principle or taking the constraint as a given when it clearly was a problem for everyone, no matter how well intentioned.

Even if a solution doesn't meet requirements immediately, it may meet them over time. It's worth identifying whether requirements are binary (meaning the idea can meet them or it can't) or whether they can be met through optimization and evolution. One of the most challenging yet successful collaborations I uncovered during my research was when Google took on a challenge to make Search— the heart, soul, and revenue generation engine of the company—"more beautiful." Google was a market dominator in the space, and the product delivered on every hard target it had, from the quality of results to response time to advertising performance. But the brand also wanted to see its user experience evolve to catch up with trends in the online space from other big brands like Facebook and Airbnb (see Figure 7-4).

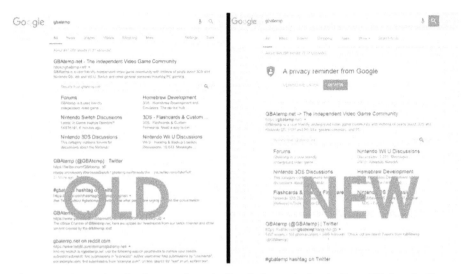

Figure 7-4. Comparing Google's search results from before and after the Beautiful Search effort

This effort, with Marissa Meyer at the helm, is well known as the infamous data-driven experiment to test "46 shades of blue" to determine which worked best. And certainly, the analytical giant thoroughly tested their options to arrive at an answer. But data-driven A/B tests weren't useful to help the deal reach the qualitative goal, which was to make search "more beautiful." Any change that the team made in service of making the user interface more pleasing negatively impacted the system's performance. And this makes sense—the old version has been refined and optimized to within an inch of its life. In the years since this effort, "beautiful search" has also been refined so that performance is stronger than ever. What was required initially was opening up the discussion about margin sizes and padding levels to engineers and product people, who had little experience with those things *qualitatively*. Jon Wiley, who led the effort, says (*http://bit.ly/2H7Djav*), "We get together, we have lunch, and we talk endlessly" so that those across the stack, from business to engineering to design, can all air out their hopes and fears.

Constraints are very often real, and they do need to be respected, but if you can help open up the team to think past them initially, you may find good solutions that remove, relax, or meet requirements over time. The sidebar "Unleash Your Imagination" offers exercises and tools to help you explore the possibilities that emerge without constraints limiting your imagination.

Tools to Help Explore Possibilities: Unleash Your Imagination

Make It Magic

One of the simplest ways to get people to let go of constraints and develop many different ideas is to encourage them to do some magical thinking. Give someone, or many people, a magic wand that they can wave when people bring up reasons "why not" instead of developing ideas.

It's important that the magic wand is used on things that could actually change, even if it might take a great deal of work. Using the wand to change the laws of physics won't be helpful, but once you can imagine what's possible if a regulation were changed or resources applied differently, it becomes easier to understand the relative return on investment (ROI) of making changes. Often we assume that changing given constraints is not possible or worth it, so we never investigate what could be unlocked if we did make the change.

Random Provocations

In this exercise, the facilitator provides random "provocations" to the team to help spur lateral thinking.

1. Gather random objects or photographs and provide one to each group or individual in the brainstorm.

2. Take five minutes to list out associations people have with the object or image. For example, if the object provided is a child's xylophone, the characteristics might be colorful, musical, tinkly, metal, and loud.

3. Choose one of the associations and brainstorm ideas based on that word. You can rotate through a few other associations, or choose a new object or image and repeat.

Figure 7-5 shows an example of how to set up Random Provocations.

Random Provocations

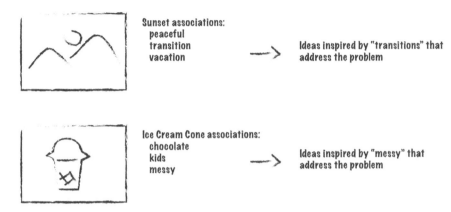

Figure 7-5. Example Random Provocations exercise

Extreme Constraints

There are times when constraints actually help people think more creatively. When teams face extreme constraints, it forces them away from typical solutions and safe ideas. Constructing ridiculous constraints also helps the team understand that the exercise is about getting "outside the box" rather than solving the problem right then and there.

Instructions for the exercise:

1. Have the group list out as many of the "givens" about the context and situation as they can on Post-its or a whiteboard. For example, if you are creating a web-based service, you might list out having an internet connection as something you take for granted. Or, if you are creating a new company policy, you might say that it will be delivered in English (or whatever the native language is). (5–10 min)

2. Next, have them take a few givens and invert them to make an extreme constraint. For example, what if there were no internet connection, or all materials were delivered in a language nobody spoke? (5–10 min)

3. Now, break into smaller two- to four-person groups and have each one spend time generating ideas using those extreme constraints, looking for unusual ways to deliver solutions. (20 min)

4. Afterward, have each small group share out their ideas and spend time together trying to make some of the ideas more practical by getting rid of the extreme constraints, but holding on to the nugget of the idea. For example, if the team decided that the new policy would be delivered via leaders acting out the new rule, maybe a more realistic idea is to have "interpreters" of the policy appointed as ambassadors to help people with questions once they have read it themselves.

As with any of the idea generation techniques shown here, what's important is to get people generating many, perhaps silly, ideas rather than focusing on one very predictable one.

Like X for Y

Sometimes creative inspiration borrows rather than invents. This exercise can help get people started generating new ideas by borrowing from old ones.

1. Create a list of well-known products and services, such as Amazon, Blue Apron, or Band-Aids. These can be modern, time-honored, physical, or digital. This is the X list. It's best if the facilitator can create this list ahead of time.

2. Create a list of key problem areas or needs to be addressed with a solution, like "customer service" or "tracking expenses." This is the Y list. This list should already exist from your assessment of the problem you are solving, but if not, the group should create it together so they understand each item. (5–10 min)

3. Have the team choose (or assign) an item from the X list (a product or service) and one from the Y list (a problem area) and have them see what solutions it inspires. For example, what would it mean if you had "Netflix" for "supply chain vendor management"? It can be useful to think through what the attributes of the item from the X list are—such as "streaming," "subscription model," "personalized suggestions"—and apply them to the new problem area. (20–40 min)

The ideas generated here will likely need some refinement, but this exercise can be useful to get people warmed up to generating ideas if they get stuck.

Act It Out

Not everyone likes to draw ideas, and not all ideas are "things" that can be captured in a single state. Getting a group to act out a scenario helps them understand relationships, motivations, and missing pieces of more complex things like systems or processes with lots of moving parts. This exercise can be used to understand a current system or process, or a future one.

1. Identify different "players" of the scenario to be acted out and assign them to people in the group; have one person be an observer and note taker.

2. Do a first run-through with everyone ad-libbing their parts to the best of their abilities. They may ask questions about what should happen or need direction about what to do at times.

3. The observer should record on a Post-it or whiteboard where people clash or act at odds with one another, indicating parts of the scenario that need to be reworked.

4. Have the group review the notes and rework the scenario to streamline it and handle clashes more elegantly.

This approach applies well to processes or policies where there's not a lot to prototype.

The Path to Great Isn't Straight

Lateral thinking doesn't follow a specific path and is hard to predict, which is why developing clear objectives and success criteria is so important. It takes leadership to make sure everyone is clear about what you are aiming for, especially when it's just out of sight. We like to think that greatness comes from meritocracy and experience, and lies on a line that slopes up and to the right, just waiting to be followed. It's often not just meandering, but mysterious. Mikael Jorgenson of the band Wilco shared his view on balancing digging in to get a "great" take versus driving yourself mad. He remembers the "Studio Response Curve," a diagram on the wall of Sear Studios (Figure 7-6), where the band recorded *A Ghost Is Born* in 2004.

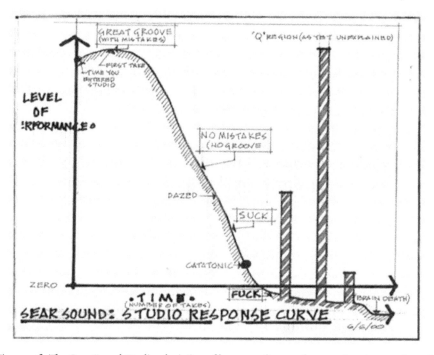

Figure 7-6. The Sear Sound Studios depiction of how recordings evolve over time (source: http://bit.ly/2IIE2B9)

The curve shows how recording may begin with something that's great but has mistakes. Over time, repeating the take again and again can yield worse and worse results. But after some amount of takes (not too many, not too few) you can break through to greatness again, this time with the kinks worked out. There's not a scientific formula for how many tries it will take to get to greatness, but given the tendency to rush through this stage in most orgs, it's usually a good idea to stick with it longer than you actually feel comfortable.

Jorgenson also shared the story of the Rolling Stones' "Gimme Shelter," a song whose bassline, to many musicians, contains a "mistake." (In the interests of full transparency, he wasn't quite comfortable with that word being applied to such a classic, but it was the only one he could find.) To most fans, however, that moment doesn't even register. He says to beware of setting up and holding to a framework whose rules and structure are so precise that it can't tolerate missteps and mistakes here and there. Being diligent about being divergent doesn't mean chasing perfection in the face of what "just works."

Often what's needed is to spend time reworking and revising ideas that have been generated a few times. It's useful to group similar ideas together, then have the team spend a session refining them, either by trying to explain them or by combining different ideas. But it's also useful for the team to have a model of success that isn't so exacting that it can't be met. The sidebar "Tell Me the Story Backward" describes an approach to get people thinking about how a solution might evolve over time.

Tools to Help Explore Possibilities: Tell Me the Story Backward

Some groups are good at generating very far-flung ideas that need a bridge back to the present for people to understand them and relate to them. You can use the template in Figure 7-7 to help people think "backward" to develop ideas as well as think through how they might evolve. Have the group place the description of the solution or the future state in the first box, and then develop a backward narrative of how that future state could evolve. There's nothing specific about the five stages to the story. Teams may need only one or two to connect the future state to the current state, or they may need more. What's important is that they think about how the idea might be reached incrementally if it's considered too radical at first.

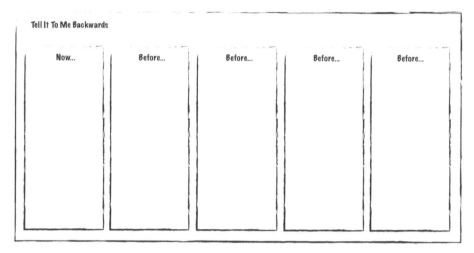

Figure 7-7. A template to work backward from an idea

Try using this technique with groups on a second or third round of idea generation to see what other ideas it spawns. Often the steps that are invented in the middle are as compelling as, or even more compelling than, the future state.

Alternatives

This exercise is good for refining ideas, or generating lots of alternatives to an idea that shows potential but isn't working in specific ways.

1. Choose one of the ideas that the group has come up with to refine.

2. List out the issues that people have found with the idea. These might be weaknesses, ways it violates constraints, or just unspecified aspects of the idea that need to be clarified.

3. Generate variations of ways to solve for the weaknesses and note down how it has been improved.

4. Lather, rinse, repeat as needed to get to something that the group feels is workable.

Figure 7-8 shows a template to use when generating alternatives to an idea that isn't quite working.

For example: If the group has a "security system" idea, you might need to add more detail to evaluate it well. You might want to clarify whether the solution is about observation, protection, or safety. From these, you might imagine alternative ideas like "guard dog," "security camera," "bodyguard," and "alarm system." Each of these accomplishes different things and takes a different form. This can help the group dial in exactly what the system could do and get at what is important about security more specifically.

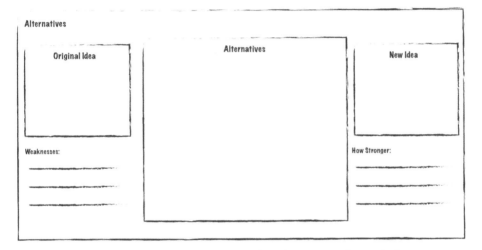

Figure 7-8. A template for refining ideas by finding alternatives to impractical or unworkable ideas that show promise

This exercise is most useful toward the end of an exploratory period, when you need to start making ideas more practical to test out.

Troubleshooting Idea Exploration

Getting the team to generate new ideas and refine them to be workable will inevitably run into challenges. This section lists some common pitfalls teams face and suggestions about how to handle them.

NO NEW IDEAS EMERGE

It's not unusual that, during their first cycle or two, teams don't actually develop very many new ideas and just try to move forward with the obvious solutions that have already been proposed. This may be because some people actually think that the solution is sound, or it may be because people are afraid to look for new ideas that won't be as workable as one that's already been identified.

So what can I do?

Third time's the charm

> At the very least, spend three rounds generating ideas in this stage. The first round is likely to be full of the mundane, the pet ideas, and some amount of performance by team members whose brains and intuition are just getting into gear. The second round will tend to push things a little further, so that by the third try, you should be covering some new territory. If you can, bring the team back a day later and try it again a few times, remixing ideas you've already discovered and getting silly with the exercise. While it's hard to call "done" on this effort, if people aren't getting anywhere new for more than two tries, you've probably exhausted that pool. If you don't feel like you've gotten anywhere new or fruitful, it may be time to invite a few new people or change venues.

Alone, together

> Most people assume that exploring ideas with more, different people means agonizing meetings or chaotic brainstorming. Those who are more introverted may dread the group environment and not contribute as much as they could. You can also let people explore ideas on their own and then bring them back as a group to share them.

Lob a stinker

> One of my favorite ways to get people to both open up and start contributing ideas is to offer up some that straight-up suck. People can't help but show you that they can do better than terrible.

Focus on quantity, not quality

I find that giving teams the explicit challenge to come up with as many ideas as possible both lowers expectations that any one idea is perfect and gets competitive types generating silly ideas just to make the numbers. What tends to happen, though, is that those people then actually come up with more expansive ideas that lead to breakthroughs. It can be useful to set a numerical target that is absurdly high ("come up with 50 ideas") or to walk around the room calling out teams or people who have high volumes to generate some competitive energy.

THE "YEAH-BUTS"

We've all met them, and they're lovely otherwise, but when you're deliberately trying to let go of constraints, those people who consistently return to, "yeah, but," lumping requirements onto teammates or spouting subject-matter expertise that isn't helpful can be a real pain. Not only is shutting down options in this stage counter to your purpose, but some ideas that don't get air time may become "martyred ideas," which can take on mythic proportions and divide groups unproductively. I've seen people cling fervently to a position, simply because no one will let them have it. This is time to be open-minded and help others be open-minded too.

So what can I do?

Make it magic

One of my favorite things to give yeah-buts is a magic wand. Grab a ruler or other wand-like object (or make it imaginary) and give the person a mechanism to wipe away troubling constraints, making sure they know they can wish them back later after they've generated a bunch of ideas to make them more realistic.

Embrace and inflate constraints

The Extreme Constraints exercise is a provocation to get teams generating ideas. The heart of this approach is to load up constraints and make them even more restrictive until people finally find ways around them. For example, if you are designing a service offering for customer support, imagine "what if" no one involved spoke the same language, or the support staff were all children. Inventing wild constraints not only stretches the thinking of those generating ideas, but it can appeal to the hidden creativity in "yeah-buts" in surprising ways as well.

Invite users into the brainstorm

While it can be a challenge to organize, if you can involve your intended users in co-creating the solutions meant to help them, often your team members will be more likely to play along because they want to impress their customers.

Split the group

If you have some people who really can't or don't want to leave constraints behind, you can appoint them to be a separate team that focuses on turning "wild" ideas into something more practical. This leverages different strengths in different groups to get a better result.

THE SWOOP AND POOP

The swoop and poop is when a senior person—like a seagull on a pier, descending upon unsuspecting folks with their eyes not on the skies—enters a collaboration or meeting halfway through, drops a few loaded comments, and then glides back out on their way to their next victim, leaving the team with a pile of crap to decide what to do with. Because the person generally holds some authority, and may even be a respected stakeholder with a vested interest, the team struggles to ignore or make productive sense of the feedback.

The swoop and poop is generally not ill-intentioned. Often, busy leaders who have expertise to share find themselves between a rock and a hard set of competing priorities. Rather than refrain from commenting and letting the team get too far astray, they want to provide "helpful" guardrails, without realizing how disruptive or uniformed their input is.

The most frustrating and challenging swoop and poops happen when the team is at the "end" of a process and the swooper rejects the team's solution entirely. This feedback might take the form of "that just doesn't feel right." This interaction can make even the most sanguine team members boil with rage, and tends to undermine the leader's credibility in ways they probably aren't aware of.

So what can I do?

Avoid it

Much of the advice out there around managing these problematic stakeholders involves stopping it altogether. Jared Spool counsels teams to use proper planning to involve these people early and often (*http://bit.ly/ 2U8EoIL*), giving them a chance to better understand the constraints and opportunities and provide more actionable feedback. While I appreciate the optimism of this approach, as someone who has committed this foul myself more than once, I'm not convinced it's very practical. Certainly you should make every effort to schedule sessions that work for people with important perspectives. Exposing them to (hopefully novel or surprising) findings about the problem will definitely improve the quality of discourse and build harmony across the organization. At the same time, unless your initiative is the *most* important one in their viewfinder at the given time, even sessions scheduled early and triple-confirmed don't mean much.

Make it useful

If avoiding swoop and poops isn't likely to happen, a better approach is to turn the steaming pile into something the team can make use of, or not. If you can exercise some empathy for the overloaded stakeholder and assume they had the best intentions, you may find that their perspective isn't as destructive as it feels. See if you can, in the moment or later with the team, turn lemons into lemonade. Walk back their specific recommendations to constructive guidance. "Make the button do X" might really mean, "make it easier for someone to know how to do X," which is actually useful input. A key phrase I use here is to follow the specific critique with, "so that the user can…" and see if you can fill in the blank with a valid objective that the executive intended.

Try being a traveling salesman

One way I've found to avoid swoop and poops being quite as disruptive, or to minimize them, is to use the traveling salesman approach, either before or after an offense happens. The traveling salesman goes door-to-door, one-on-one, to gain the necessary time and thoughtfulness required from your stakeholder. By requesting a brief session of time from them and specifically asking for their help, you are more likely to get the high-bandwidth attention you seek, instead of a performance that they may feel pressured to give in front of the group. If you don't think that you have enough pull to get solo time from an executive, you can also try the traveling salesman with one of their trusted advisors that you *can* get time from. Asking this trusted advisor to give input, or channel what they think the executive would say, may bear fruitful feedback. But it may also lead that advisor to suggest either that the executive make the time or that they themselves approach the executive to put the importance of their participation in terms that will be more meaningful and understood.

Admit failure

Sometimes, very experienced leaders have an intuition that's worth listening to, even if it's painful. As John Edson of McKinsey Digital says, "It's never too late for a good idea." When the feedback being dumped amounts to "go back to square one," it's worth considering its validity. No stakeholder (usually) wants to derail the effort in a fit of pique, so when they express deep aversion about the direction, it's worth listening.

Show them their idea

Most of my advice here can be summed up as, "don't get into a fight with the swoop and pooper." It's simply not a good idea. You lack the data to argue it, and probably don't fully understand their position. Rather than reject it, you can try to act on the feedback, no matter how wrong it seems. Jared Spool suggests taking the ideas to the users and bringing back data about what they say, positive and negative. Sometimes, even before you have actual data to share, simply showing what the person requested is the quickest way to get them to admit defeat or clarify what they *actually* meant to say.

Conclusion

When teams are seeking new ideas, they often need scaffolding to help them explore widely to ensure that new perspectives get airtime. Moving from thinking analytically to thinking creatively means that people must set aside constraints, and bring in stimuli that takes them from a linear path to a more lateral one, at times even "getting lost in the woods" chasing ideas that may not go anywhere. Give the team the time and space to come up with, and then abandon or refine, "crazy" ideas that solve the problem in unique ways.

Leading a team in this part of the process means balancing the need to keep an open mind with keeping a focus on the challenge to be solved. Because the path to the answer isn't always straight and obvious, the team must periodically stop and take stock of the ideas at hand to see how they are tracking toward the challenge.

Key Takeaways

- Teams need help thinking creatively and exploring the solution space widely to be sure to capitalize on the diverse perspectives of the group. You can employ lateral thinking techniques to free analytical thinkers up from following a linear thought process and considering only obvious ideas.

- Help the team set aside constraints when generating ideas. The ideas that get explored at first may be unworkable or impractical, but it's better to try to refine "wild" ideas than simply assume that safe ideas are the only ones that will work.

- Be intentional about separating the process of exploring widely without constraints from the process of evaluating and selecting ideas to refine and test.

8

Make Sound Decisions

Once a team has spent dedicated time exploring different ideas and getting away from constraints, they need to switch into a mode where they begin to select promising ideas to refine and make more practical. In this chapter we'll look at how teams can constructively critique ideas and manage the natural tension that arises when we start thinking less "blue sky" about all the options and get more judgmental (see Figure 8-1).

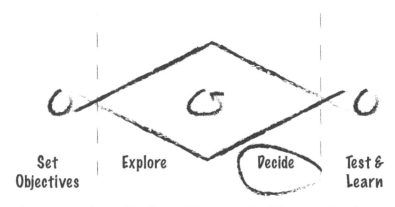

Set Objectives   Explore   Decide   Test & Learn

Figure 8-1. Exploring ideas and deciding which to pursue should happen each cycle, or even multiple times in a cycle

Democratize Discussion, Not Decisions

Chad Jennings, CXO of Babylon Health, is often brought in to make critical decisions for the company. He says, "Product management is a loud discipline with lots of discussion. I'm on everyone's email list, and I'm brought in a lot to 'make a decision.' But I'm making decisions about people who I don't manage directly and situations that I don't know intimately." He knows he should make key decisions because he's accountable, but he can't do it alone. He realizes it's important to open up discussions about ideas, how they work, and what doesn't work so that everyone understands the choices being made, and that they've been made with a great deal of thought and input.

Simply having a team vote on key decisions can be dangerous, leaving it open to pressures of "groupthink" or popularity. At the same time, leaving the decision to a senior leader who wasn't instrumental in developing options isn't the answer, either. In both cases, you lose all of the nuance and context that you've carefully engineered into the process so far.

In *Discussing Design* (O'Reilly), Adam Connor and Aaron Irizarry say, "Critique is at the core of great collaboration." For a deep dive into the art and science of giving and receiving critique, their book is a must-read. To master collaboration, there are many other aspects to consider, but critique is certainly crucial. After all, you got yourself into this mess because you valued bringing diverse points of view and skills to bear on a complex challenge. This stage of the process can be especially challenging to teams because it requires moving out of the safe space and trust you've (hopefully) established and exposing your collaboration to others. Those others won't necessarily be coached into giving "constructive criticism," and it may take some patience and effort to get their valuable feedback to be actionable. Testing concepts, prototypes, or releases with users/customers is the most typical context for this activity, where you can't necessarily explain the constraints of the problem or rely upon shared institutional knowledge to make yourself understood. But this is also where you can end the guess-a-thons and get some "truths" into the mix to react to.

It's important to look at the idea of critiquing and converging on an idea in two different settings. The first is within the group that investigated and developed different approaches together. In this situation, you're looking to bring different threads together into something coherent. Likely, if you threw away your constraints properly, the ideas you have aren't entirely coherent or plausible, so the team's discussion needs not only to praise or point out flaws, but to be generative as well. See the sidebar "Thinking Hats" for some pointers on fostering this kind of productive discussion.

Tools to Support Discussion and Decisions: Thinking Hats

It's useful to have different perspectives represented when the team is evaluating ideas and trying to make a decision. The Thinking Hats framework from Edward de Bono is useful to assign people to roles and get them to think in new ways, making room for diverse perspectives.

Assign different people different hats, or choose randomly. If you have enough people, assign several people to a color, and have them discuss different ideas wearing that color hat. The facilitator can have a color-coded Post-it or dedicated area of the whiteboard to capture the insights from each perspective.

Blue: Managing

What is the subject? What is the big-picture view? What controls are needed?

White: Information

Take a data-driven approach to identify trends and gaps. What do we actually *know?*

Red: Emotions

This is where you get people's gut reactions, either the team's own or the imagined emotions of the end user.

Black: Discernment

Look for potential negative outcomes of the idea. Think like a bad actor who might abuse the solution.

Yellow: Optimistic

Identify the possible benefits of the idea. What does it enable?

Green: Creativity

What are some out-of-the-box associations or additional ideas?

Essentially, this exercise is about channeling diverse perspectives, but it's also about getting individuals to try out different ways of thinking in a structured setting. I like using this approach when warming up a group to become more judgmental about ideas that have been generated. It can be a way to mark the turning point in the process where you intentionally shift from being expansive to closing in on things to test out.

The second setting for converging on an idea to test is in front of external, generally senior stakeholders who haven't been closely involved, but who are ultimately accountable for the outcome and therefore empowered to decide or bless the team's direction. In both cases, it's important that a healthy discussion take place, and that it be as blind as possible to power dynamics, seniority, and politics.

Make Tension Productive

Part of productive critique is going to involve conflict, and for many people conflict is uncomfortable. As children we're told to play nice; in performance reviews we hear about being too confrontational; and the business world's explicit culture is often about getting along even more than getting somewhere productive. And certainly, we don't want to turn the workplace into a toxic environment where people don't feel that they can be candid or express themselves. At the same time, if we don't have conflict, we likely aren't challenging ourselves, our teammates, and our stakeholders enough to get to great, creative solutions (*http:// bit.ly/2BVNUC2*).

Unproductive conflict is not what anyone wants or needs, but when any conflict feels uncomfortable or we avoid it altogether, how do we distinguish "good" versus "bad" ways to challenge each other? The easiest way to identify bad conflict is when it is personal, and the opposing parties are directing their criticism at the person offering an idea to the group. This type of conflict is not only terrible for the person on the receiving end of the attack, but it also generally distracts from any real discussion of the idea itself. Farai Madzima of Shopify taught me the German word *Sachlichkeit*, meaning "the thing about the thing," or being objective about discussing the merit of ideas. While Germans as a whole tend not to shy away from conflict, perhaps the fact that this word and concept is so strong in their culture also means that critique isn't seen as personal.

In *Designing Together* (New Riders), Dan Brown calls out the fact that unhealthy comments directed at a team member are often a mask for a deeper issue, one that isn't directly about the topic being discussed. When someone is attacking someone personally, rather than stating the thing about the thing, there are a few things that may be going on. First, the person may not actually understand the argument being made, and if the power distance index between the two people is high, they may not want to admit that fact. A neutral third party can restate or clarify the base argument, any necessary context or assumptions, and the implications to help disarm the attack.

Anxiety about making a decision is another reason Brown gives for unhealthy conflict. I have certainly witnessed people in the hot seat to choose a direction, having not been given ample time or information, have a knee-jerk reaction to being exposed. Often we compound this problem by holding formal sessions where the stated outcome is to drive a decision, and there's much fanfare about needing a senior leader to be decisive. Even the most real-time-processing people I have met need some time and space to wrestle with ideas; after all, that's why we gave time and space to the team to develop them in the first place! And often when someone is very decisive on the spot, that decision has little sticking power and tends to become unmade and remade several times. In such situations, it can be helpful to decouple the laying out of decisions from the decision itself.

MANAGE TENSION BY FRAMING THE ARGUMENT

In Ms. Susan's fourth-grade class, one of her principles for when she has students debate a topic collaboratively is to "have reasons." This is her way of bringing her charges back to the root of what is being debated and teaching them how to depersonalize their commentary, especially when they might have naturally emotional responses to what a fellow student is saying. She scaffolds the behavior she wants to instill by having prompts for "Academic Discussions" posted on the wall (Figure 8-2), and she refers back to them frequently to help students frame and reframe personal arguments.

She also points out that by setting up the prompts as "academic" ways to speak, she is signaling to the class that this isn't just about being nice. Teams that promote and use the correct framing for discussion—that it's about being a more capable, respected professional—will benefit more than if they simply emphasized "getting along" because, remember, we *want* friction and conflict. We just want it to be at a higher level than what you find in the comments of a YouTube video. The sidebars "Compare and Contrast" and "Model Success Criteria" offer some tips for achieving this level of discourse.

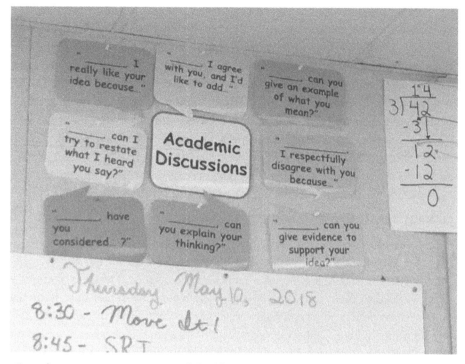

Figure 8-2. Ms. Susan's prompt to guide healthier discussions about ideas in her fourth-grade classroom

---

Tools to Support Discussion and Decisions: Compare and Contrast

Critiquing ideas often becomes freeform discourse and opinion. Take time to identify archetypes with your team and together lay out what's working and what's not in a more structured way.

1. Gather all of the ideas generated and put them up on a wall. Have the team review them all and then group similar ideas (Figure 8-3). These groups are different archetypes of solutions that can be named or assigned symbols to describe them.

Figure 8-3. Identify archetypes or clusters of ideas that can be compared and refined

2. Next, list your success criteria (Figure 8-4). Some of your criteria might be on a spectrum from high (meaning the ideas meet the criteria well) to low (ideas meet the criteria less well). Some might be more binary, where an idea either does or does not meet the criteria.

Success Criteria

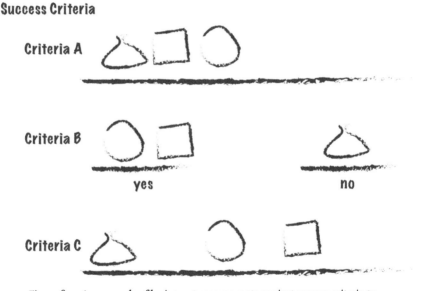

Figure 8-4. An example of laying out core concepts against success criteria to structure discussions about them

We can see in Figure 8-4 that the vase-shaped idea (#3) meets some key criteria. But it's missing one of them entirely, which makes it unworkable. You can now refine it, using aspects of the other two ideas, to "fix" what's wrong and make it work to meet all the criteria. You might also decide that idea #1 is worth refining to see if you can improve its performance on criteria C.

3. Once you have refined your ideas, have the team map the variations against the success criteria again. Figure 8-5 shows what it might look like to tackle the weakness of #3 to see if we can make it a viable solution.

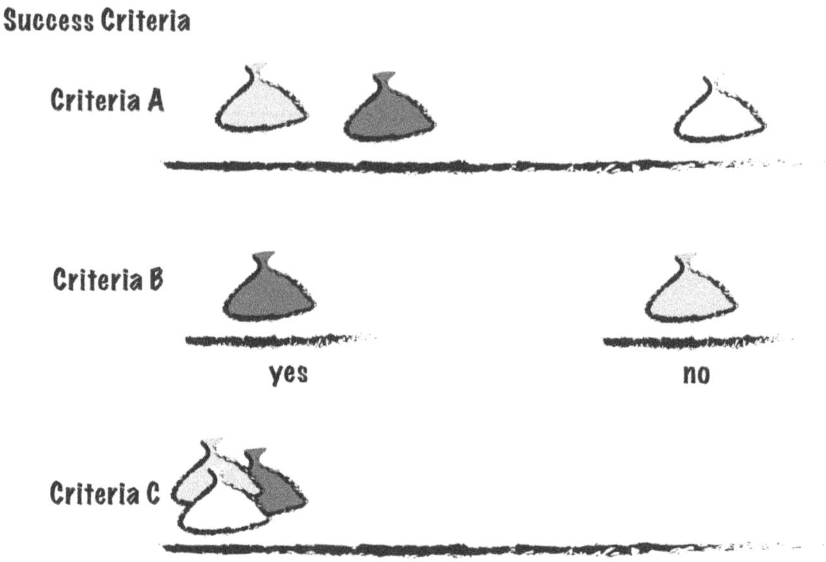

Success Criteria

Figure 8-5. Lay out refinements of a core concept against success criteria to compare different variations in a structured way

Here you can see that of the two variations generated, one has gotten over the hurdle presented by criteria B, even if it's not as strong on the other criteria.

The more you can help the team place their ideas relative to key requirements and seek to refine them in specific ways, the more you can reduce conflict around critiquing ideas and keep everyone focused on being productive.

Tools to Support Discussion and Decisions: Model Success Criteria

Sometimes you have success criteria that are interrelated. In Chapter 6 we looked at defining objectives and stating what qualities good solutions should have. At times, two criteria affect each other and need to be considered together when you're evaluating ideas. In this case, you can create a 2×2 matrix of your success criteria and have the team discuss how to prioritize different quadrants. A good test of whether your criteria have a meaningful relationship is to see if the matrix gives you a strong "no go" zone, and/or a strong "go" zone where you want to target ideas (Figure 8-6).

For example, if you're making something that's meant to be used frequently, you may want something portable. But making something small enough to carry may make it very expensive. So, by looking at these two criteria together, we can see that (obviously) we'd love to have something cheap and small, but if we can't, then what? The team discussion should be around whether something small but less cheap, or cheap but less small, is preferred.

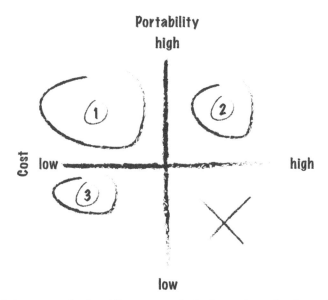

Figure 8-6. An example of modeling success criteria that are interrelated to understand what is a priority and what should be avoided

And, of course, in this situation, people are unlikely to want something big and expensive. This clear "no go" area is helpful to give the team focus, and the prioritized areas can help them evaluate ideas more clearly. Remember, if you aren't sure how people would actually make tradeoffs between different criteria, you can always ask them!

MANAGE TENSION BY TRADING PERSPECTIVES

Teams also conflict when they don't understand or value each other's contribution to the effort equally, especially under stress. Vanessa Cho, now of Google Ventures, led a team developing software for the GoPro product line, while Wesley Yun led the hardware team. The two of them knew that success depended on those things being designed and developed together, rather than in silos. But they found that across the hardware and software, and even across subgroups working on the television versus the on-device features, each thought they had the hardest job on the team. Her solution was to bring the two groups together and have them all rotate through each other's area during a sprint to understand the other group's constraints and come up with solutions to key challenges. This helped them all see and respect what the other group was dealing with, and in some cases, bring insights that made things easier overall.

Dan Brown also suggests helping teams adopt each other's perspective, or mashing up competing ideas to reach a new harmonious solution, as ways to make tension productive. I refer to this as making Neapolitan ice cream or Reese's Peanut Butter Cups, where two great tastes taste even better together.

MANAGE TENSION WITH A "DISAGREE AND COMMIT" APPROACH

Clear roles and facilitation can help groups have richer discussions and make decisions together. But there are still times when teams just can't agree and get stuck, unsure how to move forward. When arbitrating such disagreements about a decision, you may find it useful to take a "disagree and commit" approach. Patrick Lencioni's book *The Five Dysfunctions of a Team* (Jossey-Bass) describes this idea as helping people say, "We may not agree here, but in the interests of moving on, let's commit to this direction until we learn more." At this point, the best thing to do is to try the decision out and test it to see if it holds water.

Disagree and commit requires that everyone actually have what Matt LeMay, author of *Agile for Everybody* (O'Reilly), calls "look-me-in-the-eyes-and-tell-me-you-commit" commitment. In this situation, silence signals a lack of agreement, so getting people to explicitly get on board is necessary. The advantage of embracing a "disagree and commit" approach for contentious decisions is that it allows the team to air their perspectives, but ultimately asks that they remain unified in their pursuit of a direction. It can also be useful to remind the team that, should evidence arise that shows that their decision is a bad one, they must be willing to shift accordingly. Disagree and commit is a way to end debate at an appropriate point so that the group doesn't become sidetracked by the tension, or dissolve under it.

Chad Jennings says it's useful to help people pick their battles, rather than turning every difference of opinion into a "do or die" moment. Disagreements that are based solely on opinions are rarely productive. Help the team pick a direction, almost any direction, to move forward so that they can start gathering actual information about what works and break the stalemate. Jennings brought up one of my favorite phrases to use when differing opinions get in the way: "If all we have are opinions, let's go with mine." Again, the team can always change direction if the decision proves to be wrong or suboptimal, but sitting around a table arguing without any real-world data is rarely productive for very long. Getting them to agree on a direction, with the understanding that it can be altered if necessary, can alleviate unproductive tension.

Helping Teams Make Sense of Ideas and Decide What to Pursue

Humans are not rational actors, and our decisions fall prey to many kinds of biases and forces we may not always be aware of. It's important to be aware of some of these forces so you can spot them in play, and either correct for them or test less rational decisions in a real-world setting to make sure you aren't missing positive or negative options. There's been much written about cognitive biases that affect decisions, but I will recap a few you should be on the lookout for. This isn't to say you need to try to cure humanity of these biases, but if you're aware of them, you can keep track of them and test your choices more thoroughly to make sure you haven't been led astray in your decision-making.

SATISFICING VERSUS OPTIMIZING

The first tendency to be aware of is that, especially in complex domains, people tend not to look for the most optimal choice given all possible information, but instead look for the options that meet several of the most important criteria, or "satisfice." Information is often incomplete about all aspects of a choice, so we make do. Not all criteria are of equal importance, so we prioritize.

Satisficing describes the case where teams seek to meet only specific criteria to complete the work, while *optimizing* describes the case where teams seek the best possible solution. Teams looking to compare possible solutions may approach the problem from either of these two very different lenses. Be aware which one people are using when they're making choices based on different priorities, because conflict may actually arise based on that disconnect, rather than on any specific idea itself.

When you are generating ideas and selecting some to refine, keep in mind which of your success criteria must be met, and which describe the qualities of the "best" solution. Where possible it's helpful to rank and prioritize your criteria as well, especially those that are interrelated. For example, if cost versus size is a tradeoff, it's helpful to know which is more important. If you can't or don't know that when starting out, test with the actual audience to see if you can determine their priorities among different criteria as you go.

WE WANT THE BEST

In *The Psychology of Judgment and Decision Making* (Temple University Press), Scott Plous brings together several studies about how we make choices and what affects our thinking. He points out that we value avoiding loss over making gains, choosing riskier options that promise rewards but choosing more conservatively if there's a risk of loss—for example, we'd rather chance gaining $100 than losing $50. This means that we may struggle with decisions where the exact level of risk is unknown, avoiding what might be promising approaches if there's a chance of a negative outcome.

Studies also show that we value certainty over risk, choosing things that we know will pay off at a smaller rate over taking a risk. Again, if the decision being made can't be fully qualified, people may make choices based on a perception of risk, avoiding options that might have a great return and where risk can be mitigated if it's understood. If you see a team taking this course of action, talk it through and see if there's a way to de-risk more radical options and innovations.

WE WANT WHAT WE CAN IMAGINE

Our decisions are also affected by the way in which they are presented. Options that are shown with more, and more vivid, detail tend to be more credible, which can translate to more appealing. If we can imagine a scenario occurring, we are more likely to find it probable than if we can't. Plous cites the example that many people believe shark attacks are more likely than deaths from airplane parts falling from the sky. Because shark attacks receive more press than falling airplane parts, we think they will occur more frequently, even though the latter is 30 times more likely.

What this means for you is that you need to make sure that groups are evaluating options at similar levels of fidelity, and with similar attention paid to imagining how they might work. It's worth spending time, once you've generated options, to refine them so they're comparable in detail and vividness.

This also means that you can use detail and compelling scenarios to be more persuasive when you're presenting ideas. In Chapter 11, we'll look at techniques you can employ when you're trying to get outside stakeholders to understand and buy in to decisions the team has made.

Troubleshooting Decision-Making

THE POPULARITY CONTEST

Too often I've seen teams work hard to develop ideas and be inclusive of wide-ranging perspectives, only to give in to voting on the "favorite." Groupthink can be a real problem in this stage, especially among teams who don't have a ton of experience together or with constructive criticism. Unlike in the previous stage of generating ideas with no limits, what happens in this stage has consequences, and your team may not be willing to stick their neck out for an idea in case they are wrong. When asked to critique or select ideas they feel are strong, they may look to others so they don't stand out as having poor judgment or taste. Or, they may feel that making this type of decision is "above their pay grade," wanting someone more senior to take responsibility for it.

In most organizations, decisions are either made through a democratic process or by a monarch (or worse, by a monarch with the trappings of democracy). Many executives actually see their value as being someone who makes tough decisions based on their experience. Team members may pick up on signals from superiors and simply fall in line, even if they aren't fully bought into the decision.

So what can I do?

Avoid sales pitches
Jake Knapp's book *Sprint* (PCC) suggests avoiding having people present or pitch their idea. Try having people read or review the idea on their own, or have a third party present all the ideas. If someone can understand the idea without the sales pitch, there's a greater chance it's a strong one.

Host a museum tour

Along with "no sales pitches" Knapp suggests having ideas synthesized and posted on the wall with no names attached or much explanation provided. Participants can review the work individually and silently, placing dot votes or taking notes on those they find compelling.

Vote blindly

If you are going to vote, do it blindly—keep who created the ideas anonymous, and count and collect votes separately. Otherwise, when people see dots accumulating on one idea, they may add their own dot, especially if they are tired or intimidated.

SUCCESS CRITERIA AREN'T HELPING

Success is something felt rather than expressed explicitly among many groups. Even, or maybe especially, in cases where there are clear KPIs that solutions must meet, the connection between what makes a solution a good idea and the leading indicators of success may not be clear. Even if you thought you were diligent defining your objective (as we looked at in Chapter 6), you may find that once you're trying to make use of them they're just not that helpful. Sometimes this dysfunction manifests by the team allowing every idea to pass because the criteria aren't judgmental enough, or by people twisting the criteria to defend any and all ideas.

So what can I do?

Focus on the users

Whether it's a product, a service, a policy, or a process you are developing, there are likely people on the other end of your solution that will be affected. How would they define a good solution?

Map the territory, then revisit it

Sometimes you need to work backward to define success, not just options. If you have criteria that seemed useful at the start, but they're not helping you weed out and elevate ideas (and let's be clear, this is *very* common), it can be useful to look across your options to see what actual differences they reflect and then use those to move forward again. If you can develop one or two axes of qualities that your solution set fits on, you might begin to see aspects of new criteria you can use. For example, if some ideas are simpler to use but less secure, you can decide which option makes more sense and has higher value than the other.

TOO MUCH CONFLICT

Every collaboration will have conflicts, but one of the worst experiences, which often leads to groups breaking up and going their own ways, is when the conflict becomes too personal or too poisonous. In Chapter 1 we looked at what happens when conflict arises because of cultural clashes on the team. But what happens when the disagreement is about specific ideas?

As a leader and facilitator, you can help keep tension productive by helping teams share perspectives.

So what can I do?

Apply the Five-Minute Rule

At Cooper, a leading design consultancy in San Francisco, we had a rule that if teams were disagreeing about something for more than five minutes, they had to go get another person's opinion on it—anyone's opinion. This wasn't about breaking a tie or getting expertise. Having to explain the disagreement to an outsider is a great way to clarify thinking and arguments, and often the outsider made observations that no one had considered.

Swap perspectives

As Vanessa Cho did with her team, it can be useful in this situation to make opposing parties explain and defend the perspective they disagree with. Or, you can have people take on refining the ideas they dislike to see if they can improve them. What's important is to get people to worry less about the specifics of an idea that they don't like, and instead try to understand why the other person is suggesting it and what validity their view might have.

Disagree and commit

If a group simply can't come to agreement about an idea even after much discussion, it's time to pick a direction and ask the team to commit to it to gather more data and see what can be learned. As Matt LeMay says, it's key that every person explicitly say they'll commit to the selected direction rather than not voice disagreement. The direction can be selected by the person playing the navigator role, or by a leader in the group who can trust the team not to say, "I told you so" if the decision doesn't work.

Conclusion

Once you've explored ideas widely and put aside constraints, it's time to intentionally shift gears and get judgy. Teams can frame the discussion of ideas constructively, and then use constraints to make them more practical and workable. The type of discourse that you want to support in this stage is democratic, making room for the various diverse members of the team to weigh in and avoid the common traps of collaborative decision-making. Ultimately, it's beneficial to have one person be accountable for making the decision, with the benefit of broad points of view at their fingertips.

Teams that can dig into harnessing their good ideas will necessarily have tension, so don't try to avoid it. Instead, make the tension productive by keeping it focused on ideas, not their creators. In the end, you may need to ask people who disagree to commit to a direction to test the solution and learn from its intended users what does and doesn't work.

Key Takeaways

- Be intentional about separating the processes of exploring widely without constraints and of evaluating and selecting ideas to refine and test.

- Selecting ideas can fall prey to psychological biases about what we think we want versus what meets the needs of the situation. Help teams be disciplined about evaluating ideas, not simply having a free-ranging discussion of them.

- Keep the process of evaluating ideas open and democratic, but try to avoid a blind vote for final decisions. You want the benefit of many perspectives, but don't leave selecting ideas to a popularity contest.

- Critiquing and discussing ideas can lead to tension in the team. Don't shy away from tension, as it can lead to breakthroughs, but make sure it's productive and not personal.

9

Find Out What Others Think

A team that has done a solid job of gathering diverse perspectives and exploring ideas will likely have arrived at some conclusions about how they can solve the challenge they face. Great collaborators will never stop being curious to put those ideas and conclusions to the test, and will continue to seek out the opinions of other people. And while putting ideas to the test is part of a process, it doesn't have to take a long time to get to this point. Each cycle should set aside time to make sure that the ideas generated aren't just put into action without feedback about how they perform (Figure 9-1).

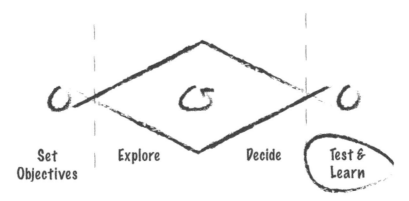

Figure 9-1. This stage of the team's cycle will give you valuable feedback, even early on in the process

Running through the process in a few days or a week and then repeating it to refine further can be more useful than spending a great deal of time trying to do it once and declare victory. The biggest mistake many teams make is waiting too long to get their ideas prototyped and tested with those they are meant to serve.

In this chapter, we'll look at why sharing in-progress work is so helpful, and how to go about making sense of the feedback you receive so it helps to strengthen ideas. Teams should be clear about how "finished" the work is that they are sharing, and present it in way that leads to actionable feedback. You'll also learn how to help team members deal with less-than-positive feedback on their work.

Share Early and Often

Matt LeMay, in his book *Agile for Everybody* (O'Reilly), says that sharing work early and often is critical for teams to succeed. Because organizations typically share finished work for a final approval, versus seeking input to refine work in progress, solutions can become inflexible, requiring specific conditions to function. When work can be shared ahead of time, before certain assumptions become etched in stone, solutions become better adapted to real-world conditions. Sharing work in progress also helps organizations continually refine and communicate their understanding of the problem(s) to be solved. LeMay told me that "having people at all levels understand what you are trying to solve for is absolutely critical," and showing solutions in progress is an effective way to create that understanding.

Sharing early and often means being curious to hear what others think about ideas even before they are fully fleshed out. Sharing also helps keep a large group more engaged in the problems and solutions at play. LeMay has found that when meeting time is used to dig into and make decisions together, it can feel more meaningful than when it's used simply to inform people of finished work.

When we find out what others think, we're doing three things:

- Turning assumptions into knowledge
- Testing ideas and hypotheses to see if they show promise with those they are meant to help
- Opening up our thinking to find blind spots and mistakes

This means that you need to help your team keep track of and be transparent about assumptions, develop artifacts that test them, and be prepared to hear answers to their questions.

Share Especially in Challenging Situations

Sharing work also tends to fall by the wayside when a team is going through a rough patch. Whether it's a release that's gone wrong or negative feedback about work, when we experience failure, it's natural to hunker down to get through it.

In *The Logic of Failure* (Basic Books), Dietrich Dörner shares insights from psychology studies about what happens in our brains when we're confronted with challenges and failure. In one study, participants were asked to play a "war game," like a low-resolution version of *The Sims*, where the player must balance different forces to keep a population safe and healthy. The game involved balancing a large number of competing factors, and the goal was not easy to achieve. The researchers found that as the game progressed, the difference between success and failure could be seen in the ratio of activity to asking questions. In other words, when things get tough, some people tend to start taking action after action without gathering information about the situation or the effects of those actions. But to succeed in balancing complex forces and make good decisions, the opposite is needed; when things become challenging is exactly when we need *more* information, not less. Communication goes two ways: when you don't communicate out, you're also not getting new info in.

As an example, Dörner looks at the 1986 Chernobyl disaster, when a nuclear reactor exploded at the atomic energy plant in Chernobyl, Ukraine, polluting the surrounding area and most of Europe with radioactivity. The engineers had decided to conduct an experiment to improve safety systems at the plant and reduce the operating capacity of the reactor to 25%. Instead, the operator inadvertently reduced the capacity to 1% by using manual controls, missing the fact that the system had automatic damping functions that also kicked in. Operating at such a low level is dangerous because the reactor becomes unstable, with irregularities in nuclear fission as a result. Operators knew that this situation was dangerous and immediately took steps to monitor and correct the resulting capacity level. Each step they took affected the capacity in one direction or another, however, which eventually led to the explosion. Dörner says, "This tendency to 'oversteer' is characteristic of human interaction with dynamic systems...We find a tendency, under time pressure, to apply overdoses of established measure. We find an inability to think in terms of nonlinear networks of causation—an inability, that is, to properly assess the side effects and repercussions of one's behavior."

We also benefit from sharing our work with those who will make use of it, even when it all goes horribly wrong, because, as Dörner says, "theoretical knowledge [of risks and consequences] is not the same thing as hands-on knowledge." The operators at Chernobyl violated some safety precautions during the event, just as we all tend to bend rules, usually without suffering any consequences for it. But they didn't "conceive of the danger in a concrete way," just as your team may not fully understand the implications of decisions that entertain a little bit of risk. Especially when what you are working on isn't a nuclear reactor, it can be tempting to just launch it into the wild rather than testing it in a contained way.

When we hunker down when things go wrong, we rob ourselves of the information and perspectives of those who could spot our mistakes and help us correct them. Sharing isn't just about communicating what works, but about helping everyone avoid oversteering and missing the nuances in complex systems.

Be Disciplined and Intentional About Sharing

Sharing work with those who haven't been closely involved is so valuable, but it also takes some effort to prepare for. Even with a group that holds different views and has different skills, once an idea has made it through the group's exploration and deciding stage, they are naturally attached to it. This idea may even be something you've asked people to "disagree and commit" to. This step doesn't need to become a huge effort, especially early on, but it also won't just happen naturally. As you begin sharing an idea that is more and more developed, it can be tempting to just start lobbing work out to an audience and assume the feedback will be useful. But to get the most out of your collaboration, it's important that you know what questions you have and share work that will get you answers to those questions. The team should also be clear on whether what you're sharing is something small that you will grow over time, incrementally, or whether you're open to actually throwing out previous work to make a new iteration. When you plan properly to find out what others think, it yields so many rich benefits; but when sharing work "just happens" at the end of a sprint, your team may get distracted or bogged down in feedback that is not actionable or leads you astray.

There has been much written on the art and science of conducting user research, and my advice in this area is simple: hire professionals to do it. That being said, a collaboration that wants to get close to users means even the nonprofessionals should get some experience understanding their audience. When doing upfront, exploratory research, in which you're being omnivorous and non-judgmental with people to understand how they see the landscape you're working in, it's important to be disciplined in your approach.

KNOW WHAT YOU ARE LISTENING FOR

The best way to prepare for research is to create (or, better, always have) a running list of questions and assumptions you want to learn more about. At the start of your project and each cycle, turn back to your objectives that say what you think will happen and why, based on what you know and what you can guess. These questions will form the basis of a plan to guide you.

A basic plan should have:

- A statement of the objective, or the part of the objective you are focused on. For example, if your objective is improving physical security at a location, and the idea(s) being tested focus only on stopping tailgating (i.e., people following others into a site without badging in), state that.

- The key questions you want answered, such as: Is the solution understandable? Will people adopt it? Does it appear to take too much effort? These are often the same questions that came up when the team was developing the idea. Review what was contentious about the idea to see what others think.

- The method you will use to test ideas out. Are you showing people example solutions in context for them to use? Or are you sharing a description of a solution in a conference room or over a video call?

- Who you will share the work with and how you will reach them. If the people you need are difficult to schedule and talk to, you should plan for that. Especially if you are working with customers, you may need to follow certain rules or enlist others in the organization to get to them.

In *Just Enough Research* (A Book Apart), Erika Hall says, "assumptions are insults," and she's right. However, since we can't know everything all the time, we can't avoid making them. What you can do is be clear and transparent with yourself and the team about just what truths you hold to be self-evident, and revisit them when you hear something that doesn't fit. Most likely when feedback doesn't match the team's expectations, you are running into an assumption that should be challenged and revised. A red flag is when a person or team begins discounting what they hear from outsiders because it doesn't fit with their worldview. If you can keep your own head on straight, you can help model the behavior of checking assumptions, and eventually get the group to police themselves and each other. Learning to get past bias is a behavior that can be learned, and it pays great dividends. You can help teams that struggle with this by pointing to or adding the assumption in your plan to make sure you don't take it for granted.

It's generally preferred to work with people one-on-one, or in realistic groups that reflect actual usage. In large panels of strangers, or focus groups, data can be skewed by participants who dominate the conversation or who express agreement they may not actually feel.

FIDELITY MATTERS

The way the team shares work will vary depending on what solutions you have and where you are in the process. From sharing rough napkin sketches with stakeholders, to acting out proposed services or processes, to creating prototypes of products to test with users, what's important is not so much how you go about testing the team's ideas, but that you do it regularly and take what you hear to heart.

The level of fidelity you show should match your level of confidence in your ideas. When your prototypes of an initial concept are polished and seem finished, people may think the work is further along than it is. Their feedback may be about details, rather than the big idea. This is not to say you should tell those who test out a low-fidelity prototype that you don't want to hear their opinions on details. But it does mean that you should focus your inquiry on the areas you are prepared to take input on. When working both with your external customers and even internally, never shut down an avenue of feedback. Even if you aren't prepared or mandated to do something about it, if you shut it down in one area, you run the risk of shutting it down where you want to hear it. Instead, take a note and move on. You can always share it with those responsible for that aspect, or discard it in your own analysis.

Be careful not to focus only on building artifacts to share without going through the expansive thinking and decision-making we looked at in the last chapter. I hear from many people, often those who are experiencing "collaboration fatigue," that "just getting something done" is a more effective use of time. If a team isn't able to come together long enough, and productively enough, to do things like set a brief or throw away constraints, prototypes are just manifestations of someone's pet ideas. Certainly, it's better to have something tangible for your customers and stakeholders to react to. As my former boss, John Edson of McKinsey Digital, says, "You can't steer a parked car," and building something is one way to get the car going. You can always pull a 180 if needed. Prototypes are a great way to learn more about how good an idea is, but it's always wise to make sure you've set some clear objectives (Chapter 6) and thought through a few different approaches using divergent thinking (Chapter 7), rather than just jumping into prototyping the first idea.

Be Disciplined About Gathering Feedback

As you prepare your plan, think about how you will keep track of the feedback you receive. If you are conducting a large-scale quantitative study, you'll likely be gathering a mix of freeform discussion and more specific, bounded questions. If the approach is qualitative, you will be collecting richer, less structured info from fewer people. Capturing these two forms of information requires different approaches.

For the more open-ended discussion, be sure to have an outline of the kinds of questions to ask, but don't feel beholden to following it slavishly. Appoint one person to be a note taker specifically for each session, and if possible keep it consistent between one or two people. Provide note takers with a script to mark up.

The key things you should look for are:

- How well the person understands what you are showing at first. Do they ask clarifying questions? Are they able to jump in and try something, or do they hesitate?

- How eager they are to try it. Skepticism isn't necessarily bad, but it can be an indication that the person doesn't understand or get the value of what you are showing.

- Whether they can use the artifact without help, or whether they make mistakes.

For more bounded data, you can ask people questions verbally or provide a survey to complete. I find that asking people to complete forms takes them out of the moment and leads to comments you may not understand later, but if there's a large amount of information to capture it may be required.

It's also useful to take images of key points or make recordings to share highlights with those who weren't there. Not every situation lends itself to this, so think through how you'll capture some of the more expressive aspects of sessions. I suggest having a checklist of images you want for the note taker so they don't forget in the heat of the moment.

One question that comes up often is about sample size. There are many different opinions about how many people you need to speak with, depending on your situation. A rule of thumb I use for one-on-one qualitative research in this part of the process is to start with five to seven people per segment (e.g., sales people versus managers) and see if you can identify patterns among them. If what you are learning doesn't seem to lead in a direction with that many people, you can add more.

Making Use of What You Learn

Because we are so used to showing only "finished" work, rather than intentionally subjecting partial and imperfect work to scrutiny, we don't have a lot of experience making use of feedback on what we create. We may have experience taking a manager's input or including subject-matter expert information, but when we expose our somewhat raw thinking to strangers or those we don't know well, we can tend to get defensive or overwhelmed. It's also common to feel like receiving anything but glowing acceptance means we've failed. Mastering collaboration means helping people get over themselves to use what they find to strengthen ideas, and to avoid face-plants caused by problems we never saw coming.

It's also a good idea to check in after every session and have the team do a quick round-up of what they're hearing. You don't want to have them drawing concrete conclusions based on the first thing they hear, but by calling out big insights, or by discussing things that should change about the way the session is moderated, the team can stay on the same page and keep things fresh.

DON'T GET DEFENSIVE

The first thing to continually remind teams testing out their work is that the feedback isn't personal. The information won't make it into performance reviews; it doesn't go on a permanent record. A better way to think about testing ideas is as an exploration to incorporate more perspectives or as an evaluation, not a pass/fail test. The idea is not to see *whether* an idea passes muster, but *how well* it works. This means avoiding talking in absolutes and focusing people to ask and hear "how well" and "why" something works or not.

Watch for team members who try to argue against feedback that's inconvenient. While it's possible that there's a study participant who "doesn't get it," it's more likely that the team member isn't understanding what seems clear to the rest of the team. Common causes of disconnects (besides faults with the idea itself) are:

Use of jargon or shorthand that isn't shared
Help teams avoid this by editing their scripts to remove things that seem to be inside baseball, especially when testing with users. It's also good to have multiple ways to explain the problem and the solution.

Failure to ground the solution in a problem
We sometimes assume that a problem is understood and experienced the same way for everyone. If the participant seems confused, try explaining the problem being addressed before launching back into explaining the solution.

Moving too quickly
Because you are familiar with the work, you may tend to rush through any context setting when sharing it. The note taker or others in the session can be helpful in applying the brakes if the person leading the session is going too fast.

I also look out for when study participants ask things like, "Can it do X?" about something the team has considered but hasn't shown for whatever reason. The tendency is to rush to explain all of the things that *aren't* in what's being tested and further distracting the participant. Instead, I coach people to ask, "Why would that be useful?" so that the discussion can stay focused on hearing from the participant.

HOW TO HANDLE DIFFERENT OPINIONS

Often people who aren't professional researchers complain that, in talking to study participants, "everyone says something different," and they struggle to make sense of what feels like random feedback or an endless series of personal preferences. Divergent feedback is often tied to key behavioral differences in your participants, like their level of experience in a domain or whether they use solutions on the go versus in a set location.

Illumina, a genetic sequencing and analysis company in Hayward, California, wanted to understand how scientists used their tools in a variety of settings, from large research labs like the Broad Institute at MIT, to small independent investigations in labs at Stanford. We visited different settings to see the equipment in action; what we were looking for wasn't about the fundamental science being done, but rather how the different environments affected the usage of the equipment. At a large organization researchers handed off samples to be processed by large teams of specialists, while in a small lab, the researchers themselves had to process their samples. This meant that the actual users were quite different in the two settings. We used the differences in what we heard to support two distinct usage modes—one for high-frequency users who were very close to the equipment but not the science, and one that guided scientists working on their own experiments less frequently. Your team should look for these types of patterns and divergences in what they are hearing and not get lost in the details of each individual user.

Sometimes feedback is divergent because people have different reasons for offering it. In writing this book I had a circle of thoughtful reviewers who helped me shape the raw material into what you are reading today. There were several parts where one person commented on a section saying, "I love this, don't change it," while another said, "I'd get rid of this." In those cases, I needed to focus on why they were offering that guidance to decide what to do with it. If you hear something that runs counter to what others have said, it's a good idea to ask why they are making the suggestion or critique.

DON'T FEAR FAILURE

Silicon Valley loves the "fail fast" maxim, which has been a point of contention for many. Most people with experience "failing" understand this to mean that not passing the test with flying colors is actually a chance to learn, not a prompt to throw everything away or become discouraged.

When I worked on a device that enabled people with reading disabilities or vision impairments to "read" text by photographing it and having it read aloud back to them, our first prototype was an unmitigated disaster. Because the core technology of the product was a camera, we had borrowed the form factor from cameras, requiring people to hold the back of the device facing what they were capturing. But while cameras are meant to photograph the world around you, often text you are reading is lying flat in front of you. As we watched little old ladies with shaking hands try to hold a heavy brick in an awkward position, we cringed. When we regrouped afterward, the predominant feeling in the room was pain and shame for having a terrible solution. The team sat with their discomfort for half an hour, but then the tone shifted. One person suggested a simple fix: to relocate the camera to the bottom of the device, making it easier to hold, and more flexible for other uses as well. Feedback may not always be positive, but it's always useful.

Experiencing failure is actually a great way to find what works, as each failure closes off an option, leaving fewer to explore. Katherine Johnson, the NASA mathematician whose calculations enabled our first trips to the moon and more, has described her role as follows (*http://bit.ly/2ECxQGR*): "We were error checkers. We did the math the men didn't want to. We were experts in error and failure. I simply kept fact checking all the errors until the only thing left was the answer."

Troubleshooting Getting Feedback

It can be scary to put work that isn't "finished" in front of those it's intended to serve. This section covers some common challenges you may encounter and ideas for how to get past them so you can learn what works, and what doesn't.

PARTICIPANTS ARE CONFUSED

During an evaluation session you may notice people aren't quite following along. That could be a sign of a bad idea or solution being tested, but more likely it's because the person leading the session is moving too quickly or not explaining things well. When participants get lost, their feedback is likely to be negative because they feel defensive or "stupid."

So what can I do?

Have a "high sign"

I make sure that in every session the person leading the discussion checks in periodically with other teammates in the room, but it's also good to arrange a signal that tells the moderator to stop and check in. This can be a simple hand raise, or it may be a verbal cue that isn't totally interruptive of the session. You don't want others just jumping in or trying to clarify; instead, let the moderator know to stop and ask questions of teammates.

Rehearse

> Do a couple of dry runs with people who aren't familiar with the effort to weed out jargon, and work on the pacing of the introduction and questions. You aren't necessarily taking the feedback from these rehearsals seriously, though you never know when a big "a-ha!" might arrive based on a newcomer's perspective.

Regroup after every session

> You can always improve the way sessions go, so encourage the team to look back together at the questions being asked and the speed of the sessions to see if there are refinements that need to be made to get better feedback. Make sure that the whole team is holding the moderator accountable for keeping things clear and well paced.

LEADING THE WITNESS

A frequent mistake inexperienced moderators of feedback sessions make is to start asking yes/no questions, or leading people by asking, "Don't you think that..." instead of leaving things more open. This is especially prevalent toward the end of a series of sessions where the team has started to see patterns and seeks confirmation rather than critique.

So what can I do?

Follow the "script"

> If you notice this behavior, direct the person leading the session back to the outline you prepared. You can use a hand signal during the session that means, "keep it open-ended," so that the flow isn't interrupted and the moderator isn't being criticized in front of participants. But you don't want to taint your findings with responses that have been coached.

Focus on asking "why?"

> Coach the team on and even practice asking open-ended questions, not just in feedback sessions with those who are testing out ideas, but with stakeholders as well. Instead of "Does this help you do X?" try "How well does this help you do X?" When the team hears feedback that is either surprising or consistent with a pattern, it's still always a good idea to ask why or say, "Tell me more about that," so that they can gain meaningful insight from the answers they are getting.

TOO MANY OBSERVERS

It can be exciting to hear directly from those you are serving, and at times there are those outside of the core team who will want to be in sessions because they have a relationship with the participants or just are very curious. It's great when people want this exposure, since it's often both inspiring and a source of great information, but having more than three people in a room can be overwhelming to a single participant.

So what can I do?

Have people watch or listen remotely

Setting up a video call or conference call for others to listen in from outside the room is useful. It's also a good way to conduct sessions when you can't be face-to-face. Since many calling systems have recording capabilities built in, this is also an easy way to record what you are hearing.

Mix it up

Have different people attend different sessions so that a wider group gets exposure to users without overloading the participant. It's important that there's consistency among those who are capturing findings and preparing to report them.

Conclusion

Just as you need to be intentional about going broad to get new ideas, you also need to be sure to share them early and often. Sharing ideas isn't so much about asking stakeholders and subject-matter experts for their opinions, but about getting solutions into the hands of their intended users to see how they actually perform. Testing ideas can take many forms, from explaining a scenario, to sharing rough sketches, to creating a prototype. Teams should be sure not to make ideas that are very rough look more "finished" than they are, so that participants don't get misled by details that haven't been thought through.

Sharing work will help you learn and avoid blind spots. Teams can mitigate the risk of making mistakes that carry consequences by testing their ideas out in a safe "lab" setting, with a small group. Be sure that you actually listen to the feedback you get and make use of what you learn, because it can be tempting to get defensive and dismiss negative feedback if you aren't ready to hear it.

Key Takeaways

- Be sure the team shares the work they do with those it's intended to serve early and often. Getting outside perspectives on ideas is a great way to find their flaws and refine them.

- When the going gets rough, teams naturally turn inward to protect themselves. It's especially important when things go wrong to gather outside perspectives and not let stress or fear lead you to simply make course correction after course correction.

- Conducting research with end users takes discipline to hear a range of perspectives and make sense of them. Teams should be clear about what they are looking to learn, and create artifacts that help them learn it.

- Just asking for feedback isn't enough. Teams need to be able to take in positive and negative feedback in a constructive way to make use of it and get the benefits of outside perspectives.

PART IV

Communicating Clearly

All can go well in a collaboration, with clear objectives, productive participation, and meaningful exploration of ideas, only for it to fall apart when exposed to outside forces. You can't expect people who haven't been involved deeply—or at all —to blindly accept information about where you are in the process, what you've learned, and what's working. This part addresses how to handle both formal and informal communications to reduce friction due to misunderstandings or poor memories.

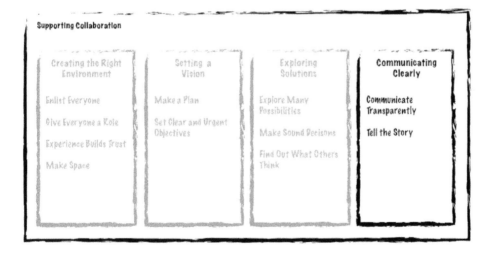

10

Communicate Transparently

In Chapter 9, we looked at the virtues of finding out what others, especially the end users, think about your work in order to make it better. In this chapter we'll look at how sharing also extends to communicating progress with those stakeholders and others who need to know what's happening and what to expect. Keeping a large, diverse, and potentially distributed group working well together requires that everyone have a clear view of what's transpired and where you're headed. Communicating clearly doesn't have to mean spending a great deal of time creating status reports, however. Instead, if you take an approach of having the right view (at the right level) into the work actually being done, and showing work in progress, you'll build trust and reduce anxiety among those who are interested in the effort but not focused on it full-time.

It can be scary to put all your cards on the table, especially if you exist in a culture that tends to regulate and gate-keep information as a matter of course. Many management structures, especially in large organizations, exist specifically to screen, package, and transmit data with the idea that it helps build a higher level of understanding. Whether or not this actually works is a topic to be debated elsewhere, but when it comes to teams working across silos and functions, relying on typical lines of communication is counterproductive since often the information needs to flow *against* the normal currents, without packaging and with a level of detail that enables deeper understanding.

At the 2013 Boston Marathon, two improvised explosive devices detonated, killing three people, causing serious injuries, and creating mayhem in a crowded area as runners all pushed toward the finish line. John Simpkins, the Executive Director of the Transformative Health Institute in Greenville, South Carolina, was one of the participants that day, and he says what he found reassuring as he and others were held at a safe distance was the consistent updates and communication from race organizers about what was going on. "Even if the message was, 'We don't have new information, but when we do, we will let you know,' that went a long way," he told me. Just as we prefer knowing that our flight will be delayed by 30 minutes versus anxiously wondering if the flight will happen at all, those in even the most command-and-control environments value knowing that the situation is being handled over wondering what's happening. When we don't keep people updated, they fill the void with their own projections and assumptions.

Simpkins takes this approach in his own work, leading many large teams to transform health care in the Greenville community. His organization not only runs hospitals and health clinics, but also engages community organizations and patients, and runs a medical school in conjunction with the University of South Carolina—all with the mission of delivering preventative care as close to patients' homes as possible to improve the health of people across the community. He feels that the only way to drive a mission that large is to make sure that he is completely open about what they are trying to achieve, and how they are performing. "If you don't provide a view into what's going on, other messages will fill the void," he says, even if that feels challenging at times. Health care is a topic that touches everyone in the community, and transforming the way it is delivered—from a reactive, ER- and hospital-focused model to a preventative, patient-focused one—can't be scoped down and contained. His mission is as much to transform the culture of how health care is perceived as to deliver it.

Simpkins learned to value transparency as a key to culture change when he was in the Office of Management and Budget under President Barack Obama, where he watched initiatives like the United States Digital Services (USDS) take shape. The USDS has changed how the government creates and maintains tools to support everything from the Veteran's Administration to the IRS, relying less on outside government contractors for such services and helping the government "do for itself again." This mirrors the journey of many companies who similarly are looking to develop more innovative solutions and fewer Band-Aids to problems as our society becomes more networked and interdependent.

This chapter looks at how you can communicate more openly to support efforts at scale, and to drive larger cultural adoption of a collaborative approach. Transparency means being able to share work as it happens, with clear context, in a way that reduces the overhead of communicating. When the team runs into the inevitable rough patches in the effort, their tendency can be to shut down communication and try to hide the struggle. Learning to be transparent even in those moments is one way to help change the culture in an organization to be more open and trusting, rather than relying on silos and barriers to hide perceived imperfections.

Transparency Supports Collaboration at Scale

Matt LeMay, author of *Agile for Everybody* (O'Reilly), pointed out to me that some companies claim to be very transparent and collaborative, and even run individual feature teams who are very effective at cross-functional collaboration and sharing at the team level, but struggle at scale to carry that collaborative approach across teams. You can see this played out in fragmented service experiences, or products with features that don't interoperate well. As each team works effectively on their own, there's less incentive to communicate with others because it's seen as distracting from what makes them a "high-performing team." Management may find it hard to curtail this behavior, because the worst offenders are often the teams who are hitting their marks. I've found that it's just as important to pressure the teams who deliver well to slow down and communicate more clearly as it is to support teams who struggle to deliver outputs. Transparency about what is happening and what's working (or not) is key to realizing big outcomes the organization wants to see happen. Teams who prioritize delivery over communicating across interdependent efforts will continue to deliver Band-Aid solutions, even if their Band-Aids might look better than the old ones.

When done well, real transparency communicates a coherent vision or plan, even all the way out to customers or users. Blair Reeves, coauthor of *Building Products for the Enterprise* (O'Reilly), calls out Adobe as a stellar example of transparency done well. Adobe routinely publishes plans for each of their product lines publicly, even if the information inevitably changes. This transparency helps keep their many interrelated product offerings clear internally and among their customers, who rely on the suite of products to create their own complex products and services. Reeves compares this approach to companies like Oracle or Salesforce, where, through acquisitions and growth, their offerings have become a sprawling set of capabilities that customers implement to solve individual problems, but never achieve the promised outcomes of improving the way the business works overall.

"MORE IS LESS" COMMUNICATION

Many people balk at the idea of being transparent not simply because it feels risky, but because it also feels time-consuming. This is understandable. When teams are working hard to deliver results, they can resent being asked to account for what they are working on, seeing it as a distraction from just getting the work done. Having to be "transparent" may seem like an additional burden that no one wants to take on. Feeling exposed and under the microscope can be draining, and once a team has a cadence together, it can be tempting to retreat into seclusion and start simply sharing that "everything is fine, nothing to see here."

To address this reluctance, it's worth looking at how expensive more typical status reporting really is. Most large organizations I've seen focus on standardized reports of different efforts, with some sort of "traffic light" rating system for how each is doing. Projects are given a green light when everything's going according to plan, yellow when issues are arising, and red when the work is behind schedule. There's little effort spent on showing *what* the team has done, and more on convincing others that the work is going just fine. The problem is that very often efforts show up on a dashboard as green, right up until the moment they turn red. Because status reporting forums are generally not troubleshooting forums, there's little incentive to rate the effort as "at risk" until it's too late to hide the problems. The sidebar "Template to Communicate Status" outlines a more effective alternative.

I've found that when you broadcast work more openly, you spend less energy communicating overall. This doesn't mean spending a whole lot of extra effort writing reports and holding status meetings. Instead, focus on always making key context and progress visible, either physically on walls or via tools like Slack and wikis. Teams should share their objectives, assumptions, work in progress, and key learnings not only for themselves, but also so that others outside the effort know where to find information when *they* want it, rather than relying on packaged status reports and status meetings. By grounding everyone in the *content* of what is being worked rather than the meta-level status, you increase the bandwidth of communication and instill a deeper understanding, all with less effort.

Tools to Help Communicate: Template to Communicate Status

Rather than relying (only) on traffic light signals of the health of the effort, it's better to frame the work in terms of where it has come from, and show what has actually been done. The outline in Figure 10-1 is one I use to keep communication of progress clear and crisp.

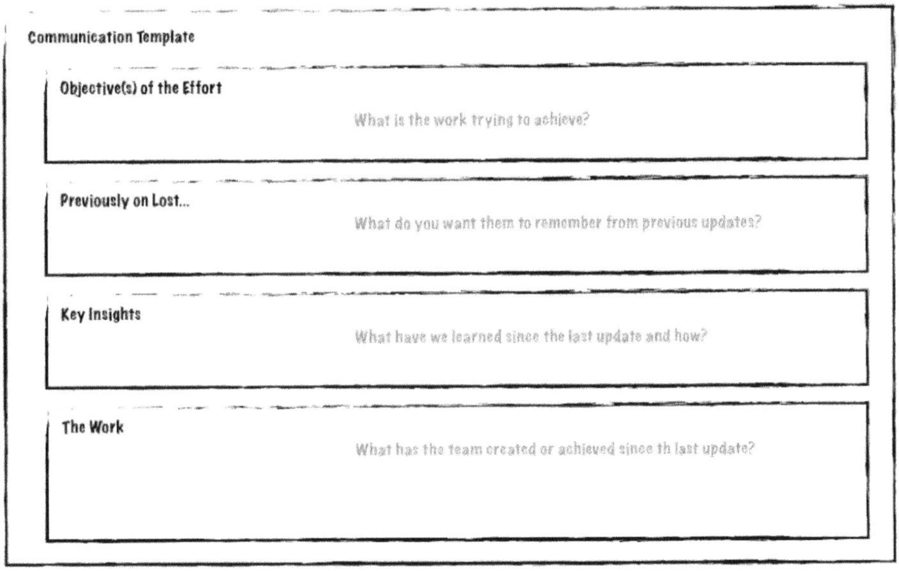

```
Communication Template

  Objective(s) of the Effort
                            What is the work trying to achieve?


  Previously on Last...
                            What do you want them to remember from previous updates?


  Key Insights
                            What have we learned since the last update and how?


  The Work
                            What has the team created or achieved since th last update?
```

Figure 10-1. A template to help you keep people updated clearly and simply

Not every effort lends itself to showing "work." Sometimes the status is more about how metrics have moved, or about developing infrastructure that on its own isn't compelling to show. In those cases, you should describe the progress in terms of what has been achieved, rather than what was done. "We consulted 14 experts," or "We completed an audit of our unit," isn't as compelling to share as, "We found three key problem areas during our audit and consultations."

Be Transparent in Multiple Modes

When your teams share information, make sure to do so in several different ways for different people and circumstances. I've seen teams who post information to a wall near where they work and consider their work done. While that's a great practice, consider that not everyone will know to look there or, especially with physical artifacts, be able to "swing by."

Emailing regular, brief recaps (one page max) of what the current objectives are, what's being done, and what's been learned is one way to keep those who aren't an everyday part of the team updated on what's happening. It's a low-bandwidth communication channel, so it won't give them deep appreciation or clarity, but it will give them the basic talking points about the effort.

Having a regular day where the team shares their work (sometimes called a "demo day") is a better way to give those who are interested a closer look at what's happening. You can do this both in person and over a video call, or even record it for those who can't be there in person. I suggest that you reserve a 15-minute block at the end of each session for questions, rather than letting people jump in while the team is sharing their objectives and learnings. Hold this meeting every few weeks or once a month, rather than having sporadic reviews when you feel ready. The regular cadence means that over time people will learn that you are always sharing, so they won't worry if they miss one. It also models being transparent for those who are used to reviewing only "finished work." Framing this get-together not as a "review," but as a view into current work and assumptions and a chance to ask questions, is critical. If you have work that doesn't "demo" very well, like some backend coding or basic research, all the better. The idea isn't to "sell" work here, but again, to give everyone a view into the work.

Posting work to walls or a shared wiki is a good supplement to the demos. Again, this isn't about packaging things up neatly. Posting a video or other recording of the demo day goes a long way. Remember to always preface what's being shared with a concise statement of what the work is focused on, how that's changed, and what assumptions it's based on. Over time, it might be tempting to think that everyone knows this information, but don't stop including it. Those who are familiar will skip it, but others will need the valuable context to avoid the "swoop and poop" approach (see Chapter 7) in their response.

Troubleshooting Transparency

Communicating "meta-level" information about the team's progress and status need not take a lot of time and effort, but it can run into roadblocks. This section covers a few common challenges teams face, and ideas about how to get past them.

THE TROUGH OF DESPAIR

Over the course of my career as a consultant with hundreds of clients in different industries and with in-house teams, there's one challenge that stands out in every collaboration. Somewhere, just after the excitement of starting an effort and the rush of learning about the problem, but just before a clear answer has been found, lies the "trough of despair." This is where those who aren't close to your efforts, your clients, your stakeholders, your boss, all start to wonder, "When will they have this solved?" Managing expectations during this stage feels scary, so the tendency is to hold back rather than be transparent because you have "nothing" to show. This is a great time to practice being open about the fact that while the effort has taken off, it's not landed anywhere yet. I used to joke with my teams that we should make sure to "schedule the fight" with our stakeholders and just get it over with. It's that consistent.

So what can I do?

Don't fight it

Plan for a dust-up with clients or stakeholders at the moment when you've finished up the research and preparation, but don't yet have the answer. Anxiety about the situation is natural, since whoever gave the project a green light probably stuck their neck out and now they're wondering if they've made a mistake. Trying to alleviate their anxiety with all of your analysis and findings about the problem is unlikely to help, and often makes the situation worse, as they see the focus as misplaced and just want you to get on with it. Just as you tolerate conflict in a team, learn to help stakeholders be resilient in moments of tension to break through.

Include the anxiety-ridden

If you are facing serious pressure from stakeholders and clients that you can't just breathe through, try holding a session and inviting them into the collaboration to generate ideas, instead of trying to present findings you don't have. Robert Bales of McKinsey Digital taught me to intentionally leave misinformation and blanks in materials at this point, just to give his stakeholders something to "fix" and be transparent about where you are. This approach also means you can enlist these potential problem people in brainstorming the solution. One thing to consider is whether this working session is best done in a more intimate setting, or if your stakeholders need a more public forum to be seen weighing in.

Entertain the obvious, but keep pushing

If there's a predictable, and maybe problematic, solution facing you, now is not the time to dismiss it entirely. You can certainly keep it in the consideration set, while still looking for other options. Arguing that the only lifeboat your stakeholder sees in the ocean isn't *quite right* won't do anyone any favors. It can also be hard to move people, especially a small group, off of a default idea.

SHARING WHAT HAPPENS, NOT WHAT MATTERS

So often, I have sat through hours of a meeting, only to find a play-by-play of the entire proceedings awaiting me in my inbox. The exhaustive style of note taking seems intended to serve those who weren't there but need to be kept in the loop. However, in all of that noise, signal gets lost. And those who weren't there are unlikely to understand or need all of the detail of a transcript. Instead, the meeting is usually held again to bring everyone up to speed on what really matters, key decisions, and open issues.

This problem isn't just limited to meeting notes, either. When you're posting work and showing progress, it's less about sharing all 75 ideas that the team explored, or verbatims from research participants, than about what the key deciding factors were or what was learned from the participants.

So what can I do?

Summarize together

When everyone is tired after a few hours of togetherness, it's tempting to split off without fully concluding and summarizing what happened. If your recorder is struggling to synthesize the group's work, make sure not to skip this step. Many meetings already conclude with "Let's go through next steps," even when the next steps are evident or completely unknown. For your collaborators, use that last 15 minutes to instead collectively answer: "What did we explore? Why? What did we conclude? Why? What do we still need to know?" Rather than focusing on action items, this reinforces a learning culture over a doing culture, when needed.

Focus on framing

Just as I've advised elsewhere in this book, whenever you are sharing work with those outside the team, don't assume they have the context of the problem being solved or the objectives, especially since those have likely evolved. I find that once you have a crisp way to frame the work, it becomes simple to post, say, or send it as a preface to ground the audience.

Capture decisions and key insights

Just as a serial TV show runs a recap before new episodes to review how the plot has evolved, you should focus on sharing highlights of the recent work. A good test of what to share is to ask: What has changed recently and why? What have we learned?

Know your audience

It's a cliché, but it's always good to think about what those around you are interested in and value, even if it's not exactly the same as what the team's focus is. Chad Jennings of Babylon Health says, "You've got to know the top one or two things the CEO cares about and address them at the start, or they will never hear the rest of the material."

THE BIG REVEAL BELLY-FLOP

You've worked hard. You've been diligent. You've got some confidence. You gather your critics, and reveal the creation. And it all goes horribly wrong. Either the room erupts in chaotic responses that are all over the place, or no one says much of anything. In *Discussing Design* (O'Reilly), Adam Connor and Aaron Iri-zarry advise you to avoid the "Ta-Da Moment" because it provokes "reactive" feedback rather than thoughtful comments that are actionable, and I second that emotion.

These moments can also be a case of overdelivering the artifacts for feed-back. Computer scientist Bill Buxton has said, "There's no such thing as high or low fidelity, there's only the right fidelity for where you are." That being said, I've seen teams struggle in this stage because they've created a prototype or other arti-facts that look very polished when the idea isn't fully thought out or is an early idea they want feedback on. When you're finding out what others think about general ideas, unnecessary detail or finishing can be distracting. You'll end up getting feedback about things that you haven't thought out fully or aren't com-mitted to, and may miss people's comments on the bigger picture. When things look very polished, your audience may assume that the core concepts have already been vetted and refrain from giving you their honest opinion.

So what can I do?

Frame the feedback you seek

It might feel intimidating to tell executives or leaders what questions you want them to answer, but I promise it is a lot less intimidating than hearing feedback you aren't ready to implement or address. I suggest listing out on a whiteboard or Post-it specific questions or decisions you need stakeholders to focus on before you share updates so they have it in mind as they take in the work. If there are people who can't seem to focus their feedback on those areas, don't fight it. It's helpful to also have an area to capture "great ideas for the future" to make the person feel heard rather than getting defensive.

Send it out ahead of time

Now, this technique can backfire, so be careful, but consider sending the work out ahead of time. The best times to do this are when you know that the work doesn't need much context to be understood. Test out whether this is the case for you by sharing it with a few people around the office first. If you don't get blank stares, you can let people spend time with the solution on their own so they can be more thoughtful and thorough in their response.

Bring them back

Because you know that "everyone" helps in a collaboration, make sure that you bring back into the process the people outside of your core team who contributed to the effort. People will naturally want to know how things turned out, and you should be sure they get to hear the story, either individually or in a group. Being transparent is more about continually communicating than it is about nailing a one-time presentation.

Conclusion

By proactively sharing information about what the team is working on, where they've been, and what's coming up, you can focus stakeholders on what's important and avoid clashes over expectations or surprises. Many organizations view project management as a series of status reports focused on whether something is "on track" with regard to a timeline, rather than the quality of the work and what the team has learned. Keeping others informed doesn't have to be a painful, time-consuming process if you focus on documenting as you go, and making it transparent over packaged status reports. It is also important to share the work the team is doing, not just meta-level information. This gives stakeholders and leaders a view of the quality of the work, not only whether deliverables are being met.

Key Takeaways

- Keep work that the team has done recently visible, and tie it to the objectives that have been set, as well as what been learned or key outcomes that have been achieved.

- Don't hoard information in an effort to save time or avoid questions. In the long run, it's easier to loop people in on what's happening and avoid conflicts over different expectations.

- While templated status reports may be required in certain organizations, giving stakeholders and leaders a view into *what* is being done can go a long way toward building trust that you are on the right track, especially when the work isn't something easily understood.

Tell the Story

In this chapter we'll look at why stories are so powerful, and what makes them work. By being conscious of how you are crafting the narrative about your team's progress, and about how solutions work in the lives of those who use them, you can help make the ideas and decisions of the group stick. Telling the story of the collaboration is as important as the collaboration itself in many ways. After all, the Post-it notes and whiteboard sketches rarely live on for very long, and seldom pack enough punch to persuade those who weren't there of the merits of the effort. In order to bring along those who were not involved, it's critical that you communicate effectively not only about what work was done, but also about the journey the team took to get there.

While we consume stories all the time, we don't get much practice creating them. When I teach workshops on storytelling, people tell me that they know a lot of the techniques and principles involved, but they don't use them at work. There's a tendency to think that the work will tell its own story, or that situations that are filled with a lot of tension will be inherently interesting and understandable. Unfortunately, that's just not the case. Great stories don't tell themselves.

When Jimmy Chin, the mountaineering photographer and filmmaker, was making his first movie, *Meru*, about the first descent of a peak in the Himalayas, he had the raw material for a story full of near-death experiences and amazing human feats. But when he shared his first cut with documentary filmmaker Elizabeth Chai Vasarhelyi to get her input, she told him it felt like watching a bunch of guys climbing; the story wasn't coming through. This led to them collaborating to use the tools of storytelling to bring out the dramatic tension and help the audience make sense of the narrative.

Without employing storytelling strategies, you might find the team experiencing a type of Groundhog Day, where those who haven't been in the trenches with the team don't remember decisions or insights that were shared previously, forcing you to rehash old material instead of moving forward. Or, you might find stakeholders and subject-matter experts getting distracted by their own pet ideas and "what-ifs" that you've already explored, and not focusing on what the team has thoughtfully prepared.

The art of storytelling is a field of study unto itself, but for the purposes of better collaboration, there are some basics that will go a long way toward helping you get buy-in and establish a clear direction for the group. For this chapter I owe a huge amount to Christina Wodtke, author of the best-selling book, *Radical Focus* (Cucina Media), who shared her thoughts on storytelling and what makes stories work. As with many topics Wodtke speaks and writes about, her notes on storytelling were well researched and articulated, and helped me put my own thoughts and experiences with storytelling into a more organized—and hopefully useful—format.

Why Stories Are So Powerful

Stories are universal, so we respond to them automatically because we are literally built to hear them. Kendall Haven is a leading expert on the neurological and cognitive science of story, and his book *Story Proof: The Science Behind the Startling Power of Story* (ABC-CLIO) looks at how our brains process stories, and shows some surprising evidence that we are in fact hardwired for them.

When we listen to information, even before it reaches the conscious mind, our brains turn it into story form within what Haven and his researchers call a "neural story net," a dedicated part of the brain that processes stories and operates on a "make-sense mandate." This mandate means that our brains will make sense of information as a story, and what we can't make sense of, we ignore or distort. Because our brains process such a huge amount of information, this is part of how we keep from being overloaded. Haven's research shows that we will even reverse or invent key data points in a narrative if they don't fit with the sense-making our busy brains are trying to do. In a video about the topic at Stanford (*http://bit.ly/2UcgZAd*), Haven gives a few entertaining examples of how our brains do this.

So, if your audience is sitting there inventing their own information and creating their own stories in their busy brains, what hope do we have of convincing and informing others of what we said and did? It turns out that by using effective storytelling techniques, you can minimize that distortion and keep your audience on the same page.

Elements of Storytelling

Most experts agree on the basics of storytelling, even if they use different names and vocabulary. These include elements like the story arc or structure, characters, and mechanical details like dialog and exposition. While the topic of storytelling is itself very large, I will touch on just the key elements you need to master to help collaborations make a bigger impact on your audience.

The first critical element for our purposes is the story arc, or how the story progresses. This may seem obvious, and yet, in a business setting, this element is often the first to go. In an effort to be concise and (we imagine) dramatic, presenters often unveil a big point or takeaway, and try to back it up with data as an argument. I noticed this early on in my career when delivering my own research findings to clients. I would create these utopian "stories" about how easy life for people would be if only they had a great new product. After a few failures, I made sure I always included an "oh shit!" moment, where the protagonist faces a challenge, and *then* the great new product or service makes an appearance to save the day.

Consider telling *The Wizard of Oz* the way most business presentations go:

A young girl wakes up and has newfound respect for her family.

There's no tension to make people care about the girl or her family, nor any understanding about why she maybe didn't respect them beforehand.

But adding that tension is only one piece of the puzzle. To be effective a story needs:

1. An *inciting incident* that kicks off the action. For a collaboration, this is usually a business objective or hypothesis that the group can or will agree is desirable. It can also be a problem that the group faces that needs to be addressed.

2. Next, there should be a *struggle or failure* that the "characters" or collaborators face. In a collaborative setting, this might be a description of pain points observed in research, or ideas that were tried that didn't work out. This is where the "oh shit!" moments come in.

3. The *climax* of the story is where we unveil the idea or insight or product of the struggle that the team has developed. Instead of opening with your big idea, by leading up to it with some struggle, you've engaged your audience

in wanting to know and embrace the winning idea rather than pick it apart for no good reason. The climax should bring the audience to understand not just *what* you did, but *why*. You should show the criteria and values you discovered and used to find the solution.

4. Finally, your story must have a *resolution*. The happy couple lives happily ever after or, more likely in our case, there are some next steps or key indicators that we need to watch to see how well we did or to create the solution.

All of these factors are important, because they're what gives the story its neural-net-inducing powers. As the story moves through each phase, our brains fill in (or remove) details so it will make sense to us. When you shortcut a stage or put them out of order, your audience is now suddenly writing their own version of the story in their heads, and you are no longer in control of what they might take away from it.

Using story structure doesn't mean just delaying the big reveal of your idea behind a lot of prelude. A team of young people I once mentored was developing a medical device that had some tricky mechanical elements to be worked through. The team diligently identified all of their constraints and prototyped over 70 permutations of the mechanism to see how they could make it smaller and easier to use. Their presentation showed some of the more interesting of these, and it turns out many of them were interesting to the team for one reason or another. Their big idea made an appearance somewhere after slide 50 of their presentation. Instead, we worked on four or five slides that talked about the process and criteria they used that made it challenging and required 70 prototypes. We painted the story as a mystery to find a needle in a haystack of possibilities, rather than an exhaustive catalog of prototypes. "Show your work" may be great for math problems, but it kills stories. For more advice on using the storytelling elements to make the narrative of your work compelling, see the sidebar "Storytelling Worksheet."

Storytelling Worksheet

While the elements of storytelling might seem obvious, it isn't always easy to create a story out of thin air, especially when the team has been focusing on finding and explaining a specific solution to try out. The framework in Figure 11-1 can help teams generate explanations that don't simply focus on the positive side of their work, but make sure to address the problem and struggle that makes a story compelling.

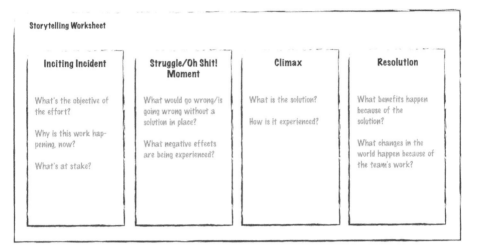

Storytelling Worksheet

Inciting Incident	Struggle/Oh Shit! Moment	Climax	Resolution
What's the objective of the effort?	What would go wrong/is going wrong without a solution in place?	What is the solution?	What benefits happen because of the solution?
Why is this work happening, now?	What negative effects are being experienced?	How is it experienced?	What changes in the world happen because of the team's work?
What's at stake?			

Figure 11-1. A template to aid teams in creating simple stories to communicate in ways that stick and keep people engaged

The "Oh Shit!" Moment

The biggest mistake I see people make in the workplace when trying to be persuasive and engaging is forgetting the very thing that makes stories sticky—suspense. Or, as I call it, the "oh shit!" moment. When I first began using scenarios and stories to compel executives to understand and support new product and service strategies, I would often focus on how great the offering would be, and how it would improve life for those who used it. My stories showed a person going through their day, experiencing no problems, all due to our great invention—aren't we smart! But I began to notice that no matter how finely crafted I made my presentation, I was often met with a "so what?" response.

One day, after a particularly unsuccessful set of sessions getting feedback with customers, I found myself sharing the difficulties we were having, and how they had changed our thinking about how the product was used. I noticed that the executives were much more engaged than usual, because here, I finally had a real story where *something happened*.

It can be natural to try to exclude the "oh shit!" moment in an attempt to focus on the positive—the successes. But when you do, the opposite happens. With nothing to compel their curiosity about how the story will turn out, the tone and emotional tenor of the conversation is flat and uninspiring. This doesn't mean you have to air every bit of dirty laundry outside the team, but it does mean that you should always make sure you include a struggle in the story that your solution helps your protagonist overcome.

The Shape of Stories

The elements of story—an inciting event, a struggle, a climax, and a resolution—can also take different shapes. Not every story behind a collaboration needs to be an epic tale from a storybook. There are two major shapes that stories take in the business world (Figure 11-2).

Story-Decorated Update

Story-Driven Struggle
That's Been/Could Be Overcome

Figure 11-2. Stories tend to show up in two basic shapes in the business world

Each story shape does a different job and can be used in different situations:

Story-Decorated Update

If you're looking to keep a group of stakeholders informed of and confident in your efforts, the Story-Decorated Update is an effective way to tell different vignettes that punctuate your overall delivery of information to a group that needs continuity. The key is to give each of these stories their own struggle and climax in a concise manner.

In her essay "Working with Story" (*http://bit.ly/2SxJAhM*), Christina Wodtke describes the "story-decorated" approach, where the arc follows a central theme punctuated by several smaller stories. She identifies Ken Robinson's TED talk

"Do Schools Kill Creativity?" (*http://bit.ly/2HamSdl*) as a shining example of using multiple different stories to make a larger point (Figure 11-3).

Just because the nature of the meeting is more of an update, or a report, it need not be a dry recitation of the facts. The trick with being story-decorated is ensuring that you aren't just stringing together different anecdotes and treating them like a spray of facts to dazzle you audience. Instead, you need to think of arranging your "mini-stories" into their own arc that brings the audience along.

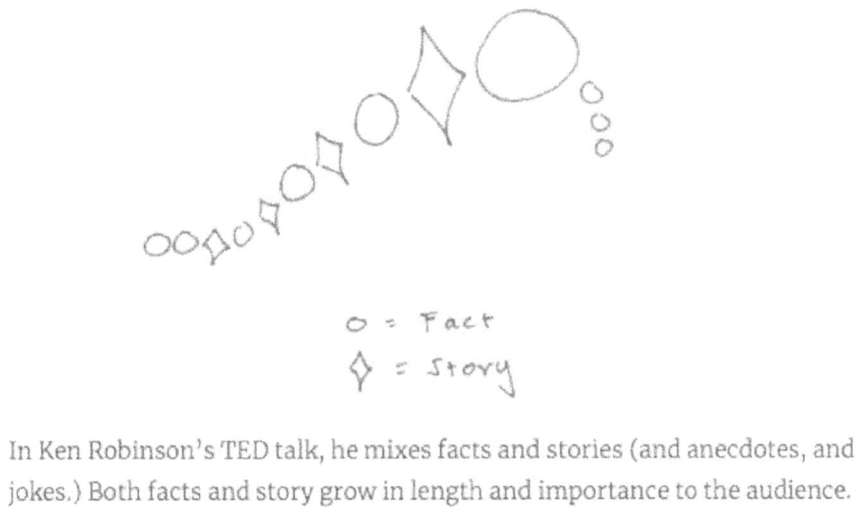

In Ken Robinson's TED talk, he mixes facts and stories (and anecdotes, and jokes.) Both facts and story grow in length and importance to the audience.

Figure 11-3. Christina Wodtke's depiction of a story-decorated presentation

The Story-Driven Struggle

If you are looking to create buy-in, the Story-Driven Struggle structure can be an effective way to pitch bold new ideas, or present a synthesis of lots of prespectives. You can help create buy-in to an initiative by ensuring everyone can relate to a narrative that pulls facts into something memorable.

This shape serves to ground the audience in the pain points—the struggles of someone in the target market who goes on to achieve greatness, with the help of your solution. This is frequently employed in business in the form of demos and proposals. Steve Jobs was a master of the pitch form in his onstage presentations at Apple events. He tended to minimize the "hurdle" aspect of the pitch in favor of dazzling audiences with clear, impressive images of a brilliant future.

Mad Men's carousel scene (*http://bit.ly/2T3Uyk6*) is an exemplary, almost meta-level "pitch about pitching" that nails the form.

Whichever approach you choose, if you bear in mind the overall shape of your story and make sure to create tension to move the audience through, you'll be much more successful. You will rely on the specifics of a story, whether one or many, to carry people through your presentation. You aren't writing a novel here, but it's still worth thinking through factors like the setting of the story, and how you foreshadow struggles and problems in order to engage people's neural networks. The sidebar "The Mechanics of Stories" gives additional tips for effectively moving an audience through your story.

The Mechanics of Stories

In any good story, it's the details and the techniques that the writer uses that transport us through the story's structure. The mechanics of your story will support (or detract from) the main message you want to convey and the experience you want your audience to have. "Mechanics" here means the specific techniques you use to bring the plot to life, help people connect with the characters, and communicate where you and your collaborators are in your journey. Mechanics in storytelling is a big topic, so I'll focus here on those that are most relevant to the kinds of stories you are likely to tell.

It's also important to note that for our purposes, the stories we tell are unlikely to be simply written prose. Most often you will be working in a more oral tradition, speaking to an audience about what you saw or what you envision. This means that you have the advantage of using visuals and performance techniques in your delivery.

Mechanics can refer to:

Setting/place

Bring your audience into the location that supports the drama. If it's somewhere interesting, spend time telling (or better yet, showing) what it looks and feels like. When I did research with child diabetics in their homes, it was crucial to show how their houses were both similar and different from what's common to make the audience understand where they needed help and where they needed to be respected. Conversely, when your story is about the team or takes place within the office, make the setting drop away to focus on what the audience isn't familiar with.

Cadence and pace

Think about how quickly you want your story to unfold. Make sure you have enough time dedicated to building up tension and suspense, rather than jumping straight into the action. Repetition grounds people using a key phrase or image, bringing them back to a point or moment. Pausing, or bringing friction into the progression ("but we were stopped by..."), makes the audience wrestle with an unforeseen challenge.

Point of view/tense

Be deliberate about choosing to tell the story in the first, second, or third person. First person lets you speak very convincingly, but it also tends to minimize the group effort. Third person is the most common point of view I've seen in the type of persuasive stories used in business. Demos are best done in the third person if the audience doesn't fully understand how their target market differs from themselves. Use second person sparingly, as your audience probably tends toward taking a self-centered view, which your collaboration is there to disrupt. While it can be useful in a "how-to" situation (much like I've done in this book), in most stories the second person is tricky, and many editors and writers counsel against using it. Note that Steve Jobs often used the second person in his performances, because the Apple story aimed for a sense of universality where everyone brings their own viewpoint. Choosing to tell the story in the past is great when you are recounting something that has occurred (obviously), but the present tense is better when you're demonstrating prototypes or features. The future tense can be effective when the goal is to draw the picture of a brave new future or a rebirth.

Reversal and foreshadowing

As a storyteller, you can use your audience's preconceived notions to your advantage. A reversal is when you turn something that is taken for granted on its head. Liz Ogbu, in her TEDx talk, "Why I'm an architect that designs for social impact," tells a personal story (*http://bit.ly/2TkZD6N*) about her work by opening with, "I'm an architect, but I don't design buildings," piquing the audience's curiosity about what that means. Foreshadowing refers to dropping clues about what will happen based on the audience's expectations. *Chekhov's gun*, the idea that "if a gun appears in the first act, it goes off in the third act," is the most common example of foreshadowing. Foreshadowing taps directly into the neural story network that Kendall Haven describes, using the brain's natural tendency to make connections between events to make sense of them. One useful trick is to start a story where everything is going along swimmingly, when you tell the audience directly that all is not as it appears and a villain is lurking somewhere in the future. This keeps people on the edge of their seats, looking out for the danger. Foreshadowing is a form of mystery, or whodunit—one of the most popular forms of stories we consume today.

Conceits and metaphors

Another technique you can use to make your story stick is to draw a comparison to something else that will highlight contrasting or similar aspects of your big idea. Danielle Malik's talk about using data to develop products (*http://bit.ly/2XvZCfu*) compares it to being in a bad relationship. Instead of a more straightforward, "I used to think X, but now I think Y" formulation, her conceit injects humor and describes how designers can be seduced by the idea that data, despite its imperfections, offers something perfect. Be careful that you know your audience when using this approach, or it might seem overly precious.

Delivery

Finally, consider the actual telling of the story itself. Where will it take place, who will be delivering it, and what else will be done in that session that will support or contrast with your main point? A good place to get practice with creating and telling stories is during demos or other reviews of a finished product. This is where the collaboration has already taken place, so trying to ask for feedback or participation is disingenuous. Rather, the best thing you can do at that point is use story to bring the audience along on the journey you have already traversed.

Laddering

When choosing a shape for your story, it's also important to establish a core concept of the story at several levels. Laddering is a technique you can use to help you create that concept, and stay organized when you are presenting and discussing the concept with others. Laddering means taking the big message you want to convey to your audience through multiple levels of abstraction—from the very abstract to the concrete, and even back again. Steve Jobs was famous for his product demos at Apple conferences. His presentation of the first iPhone is a classic example of starting with an abstract concept: a new type of mobile phone. Then he moves into the three big things that make it different: it's a phone, a music player, and a camera. From there he describes specific features, and then he demos how the iPhone works. This helps people understand something new both as a big idea and as a set of specific features. You can invert the approach as well, starting with specifics that people may be familiar with or looking for, and leading up to a bigger idea or rationale.

I find this technique useful not just in creating the story, but also in telling it, especially if you aren't entirely comfortable in front of an audience, or you're facing a tough crowd whose interactions during the session tend to put you off your game. While presenting, you've probably experienced the situation of people jumping into your well-crafted spiel with questions that seem out of place, are overly detailed, or force you to restate something you *just* said. These people generally aren't trying to derail the discussion; rather, they're trying to fit what you're saying into their neural story net. So you need to be able to allow interruptions and requests for clarification without losing the plot entirely.

Take the situation where you are speaking broadly about the concept at hand, at the abstract level, and someone asks about a particular edge case or technical detail that seems very remote from where you are at the moment. Perhaps, and hopefully, it is something you were going to address, but at a different point in the presentation. The trick is to pause and take a moment to climb down your ladder of abstraction to the detail level—moving, say, from Food to Cows to Tacos to Best Taco Toppings—to share the secret you were saving for later. But at this point many people may find themselves stuck: *What was I saying before I got derailed?* By having the ladder of your concept in your head, you can climb back up the rungs to your higher-level point about cows as a source of great nutrition or, for non-meat-eaters, the merits of eating plant-based sources of protein and saving the cows. Likewise, when you are deep in the details and someone expresses skepticism or confusion about the big picture, traversing the ladder helps you quickly restate the big idea and then move back to your detailed point. See the sidebar "Laddering Template" for more advice on structuring a ladder for your ideas.

Laddering Template

It's useful to have the team level up their ideas from a conceptual perspective to a specific one. Not only will this help them explain the idea, but it also helps the person presenting it when they get distracted or interrupted while speaking. A ladder (Figure 11-4) moves from the most abstract to the least and back again.

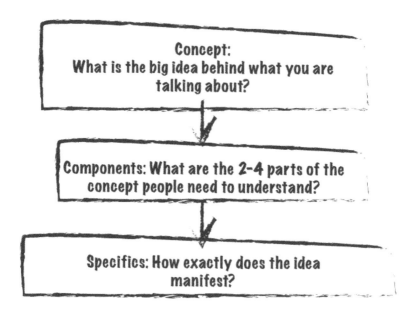

Figure 11-4. The laddering framework

What a Character!

So far, we've been talking mostly about the structure and ideas that a story needs to communicate. And, since this isn't a book for novel writers, we've generally been talking about using stories as a way to make more persuasive arguments in business settings. So, it's worth talking about the "protagonist" and characters for that context, because it's unlikely that the stories you tell will take the form of tales told 'round the campfire. More likely they'll be artfully constructed and delivered examples that support your argument. You don't have the time or license to spin up backstories for what we might think of as characters.

So what does "character" mean in this context? There are three main types of characters that storytellers in the corporate world use: end users, team members or employees, and brands. Focusing a story on end users is great when demoing or proposing features for them. It sounds obvious, but you'd be surprised how often people make the "user" in a scenario an unspecified ghost of a person, giving little thought to their motivations, challenges, or goals. Some people think that by creating this sort of person, they are addressing a wide set of users, smoothing out the differences in target markets in an effort to show how the solution meets a wide audience. And they'd be wrong. Without understanding what drives the character, and what makes them different from "everyperson," you run the risk of your audience inserting themselves into the story and bringing into the mix all the preconceived notions you worked so hard to get past.

The second type of character to consider basing your story around is the team or employees involved in the collaboration. This approach works best when you need the audience to understand the challenges a team faces, or to give the "status update" a more persuasive edge. I've also focused on team members as characters when I needed to convince stakeholders of a perspective shift the team has experienced. As I mentioned in Chapter 9, I was once part of a team that was developing a device to enable nonsighted or dyslexic people to photograph and "read" text via their ears, and our first prototypes mimicked the form factor of a camera. Once we started seeing actual users struggling with something intended for a completely different usage, we realized we needed to go back to the drawing board. No one wants to give *that* status update. Instead, we focused the narrative of our progress around our initial enthusiasm for such a strong, iconic form, followed by our despair upon seeing that form fail utterly, and finally our redemption in what a better solution would be—with a nod to the fact that we'd need a bit more time to make new prototypes. Rather than experiencing the backlash of a missed milestone, we got nods of agreement that we were on the right track. When what you seek is empathy for the team, put them at the center of the story.

Finally, putting the brand at the center of a struggle and success is the meat and potatoes of the advertising industry, but that trick doesn't belong to them alone. Think about BMW, the "Ultimate Driving Machine," setting itself up as a

James Bond–type character that is highly capable, pleasurable, but never too finicky to tackle an adventure. Or, take the Method brand of household products, which, at launch, positioned itself as the answer to other types of cleaners, calling them "dirty" in comparison. A brand need not only be the company or product brand, though; teams can brand their own work and tell the story of what they accomplish through that lens.

Note-Taking Supports Storytelling

Often, storytelling is left until the end of a cycle, when the team is furiously pulling together the output of the collaboration, and there isn't a great record of what happened along the way. One suggestion is to have the team historian keep explicit track in their notes of the story as it unfolds to make creating the narrative easier. I use a system of symbols (Figure 11-5) in the margin of my notes to help me find sources of friction, big breakthroughs, and quotes later.

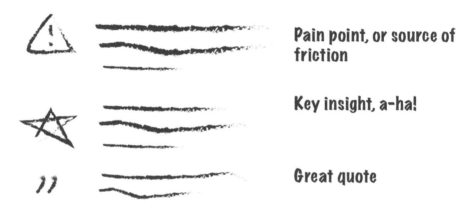

Figure 11-5. Example notations I use when taking notes to help me go back later to pull out specifics for the story

Try not to leave the story creation until the very end. Teams can take time after every few sessions to talk about what story they would want to tell so far, which not only will help the person writing it, but also serves to keep the team united in their view of their own progress.

When creating a narrative, teams may struggle with how much of their story is nonfiction. There may be a bias to want to be fully "authentic" about what actually happened, or didn't. I like to coach teams to think about their tale as revisionist history, where the main plot is a solid reflection of the takeaways that the team has come up with, even if some of the events have been altered for dramatic effect.

Over time, you may find that your story is actually episodic, where you are telling it as it unfolds in a series of meetings. In this case it can be useful to practice what's known as *retconning* the story, short for "retroactive continuity." This happens often in comics and movies where stories typically are long-running with multiple authors. A classic example of this is when Sir Arthur Conan Doyle brought Sherlock back from the dead after having him killed off by his arch-enemy, because fans clamored for more tales. *Star Trek* and the race of Klingons is another example: their appearance and storyline change dramatically over the 40+ years of the show, but unlike in many retcons, the storytellers barely acknowledge the changes, instead relying on the audience to trust the narrative.

Troubleshooting Storytelling

Creating compelling stories may seem like something that happens naturally, but teams often don't spend the time to do so. This section details some common pitfalls that storytellers run into, and ideas to avoid or recover from them.

NO STRUGGLE TO THE STORY

Teams may find it hard to expose anything negative about the collaboration. This leads to nonstories that fail to engage the audience. Leaving out the struggle of the main character, or a failure the team faced, is a surefire way to fail. Remember, without an "oh shit" moment, it can be hard for the audience to relate to the challenge and start them jumping into their own ideas.

So what can I do?

Invert it

> If all you have are sunny moments and you can't think of a struggle to present, write about the opposite outcome happening. You can present it as a potential future that never happened, that you avoided, but it will start you thinking about what the team actually overcame to get to the positive outcome.

Take notes

> Make sure you identify someone on the team whose responsibility is to find the negatives—the struggles—and bring them to life.

Test yourself

> If you think all you have are right answers, there's no better way to create a struggle than to put your solution in front of others. When they develop arguments and poke holes at your ideas, you can turn that into fodder for a better struggle to overcome.

INCONSISTENT AUDIENCE

No matter how good your story is, it can be challenging when the people you are telling it to are coming in and out of the storyline. Whether it's someone who leaves the room to make a call, or audience members who attend different sessions over time, missing episodes in the progression, you can find yourself skipping around and losing the plot.

So what can I do?

Previously on Lost

> If your story is unfolding over several sessions as the collaboration progresses, make sure that you recap what you've told people in previous sessions. This should be short, sweet, and focused on relevant plot points and characters needed for the part you will tell that day.

Have a private audience

> If you know you have a key player who missed an important session, try to meet up ahead of time or afterward to catch them up. Don't just leave them hanging with a hole in the story, or they will fill it in themselves.

Record it

> Whether it's a written recap or a video of the presentation, you can make your stories available offline in case you need someone to relive it. If you can, include the debate that the story provoked so the audience can hear when their questions or arguments are raised and addressed.

Conclusion

The work you do as a collaborative group can reach breakthrough ideas and mitigate risks to deliver great solutions. But don't take it for granted that everyone will understand and follow what you do. You need to be thoughtful about introducing a challenge that is overcome, to engage people's neural networks and to keep them from inventing their own information or relying on wishful thinking.

Being intentional about telling a story that places the team or intended users at the center helps avoid a mistake that designer Mike Monteiro calls "real estate tours" (*http://bit.ly/2SxPxev*) of the solution. Many people fall back on just listing out elements of the solution, without tying back to why those elements are there and why they are good.

Christina Wodtke says that sharing the journey behind the team's work is as important as the work itself: "If you have a successful product it's important to tell those who will copy you what to do, and what not to do. Tell people what you screwed up and teach them to make better decisions. It's not always about the facts, but about the greatness of the story."

Whatever you decide in terms of how to tell your story, by tapping into the neural story net of those who weren't closely involved in the collaboration, you will increase your chances of success and buy-in.

Key Takeaways

- Our brains are hardwired to understand information in the form of a story. By taking a little time to create a narrative about what's been done, you will get a more engaged audience that better understands the team's effort and progress.

- Good stories don't just happen, even if the events they cover are very dramatic. They have a structure that takes the audience through a struggle and shows how it has been (or is being) overcome. It's a common mistake to be overly optimistic when we share the work we've done, leaving out the struggle in an effort to impress, which can backfire.

- If you craft your story to work at different levels from the most concrete to the most abstract and back again, it will be easier to give presentations without getting lost.

- Stories that the team tells can focus on the end user of a solution that's been created, the team itself and what they are learning, or the brand and how it's supported by the work being done.

- Be sure to take notes as you go about what's happened in a way that supports storytelling, so that you don't forget about the struggles and eureka moments that make up a great story.

Conclusion

Becoming a master of collaboration is a journey worth undertaking, and I hope that by now you've seen some ways that you can bring people together to do great things. If you face enormous challenges or risky, intimidating situations, there's no better tool to have at your disposal than a great group of people willing to tackle them with you.

In this book, I've made the case for collaboration as the approach to solving problems that are complex and confusing. The saying at the beginning of this book, "if you want to go fast, go alone; if you want to go far, go together," speaks to the support that we give each other when we work well together. I've shown how it can help your professional endeavors, whether you are creating innovative products, saving lives in the ER, or reinventing how your organization works. But collaborations shouldn't be thought of only in our professional lives.

Jim Kalbach, author of *Mapping Experiences* (O'Reilly), shared a story about a collaboration he was part of in 2017. Kalbach was approached by Hedaya, an organization dedicated to countering violent extremism, to lead a collaboration to understand the journeys of former extremists who had left their pasts, and see how their experiences could be leveraged to reach others like them. He flew to Dubai and met a diverse group of people, including former gang members, Islamic extremists, neo-Nazis ("formers"), as well as the US State Department and NGOs, over several days of collaboration where formers explained aspects of their lives that were previously invisible to their partners. By holding a safe space where all were respected, the group began to understand what turns people away from violence, and how their identities suffered once they were on the outside. After spending a lifetime understanding themselves in opposition to an "other," formers faced depression and isolation that made it tempting to return. In the end the group came up with actionable steps that they could take to recruit, support, and train formers to become agents of change to reach more violent extremists and change their perspectives. "I don't know how else that diverse a group could have gotten together except at the UN," said Kalbach, "and that setting is where people just speak to each other about this topic, as they had in the past." Collaboration enabled them to have a space where emotions could be allowed into the discussion, where people could trust one another and listen to one another's perspectives, and where they could ultimately develop new ways of thinking about a vital problem we all face.

Throughout my career, my greatest accomplishments and most enjoyable experiences have happened while working closely with people very different from myself. I've learned to be humble, and to make what I think are brilliant ideas into solutions that actually work. I've learned to see the world differently through clashes in perspectives. I've laughed, I've cried, and most importantly, I've made lasting relationships with people of all kinds, who continue to be sounding boards and inspirations in my life and work.

It is my sincere hope that by employing some of the approaches I've gathered here, based on a wide range of experiences, you too can take the experience of working together from "It's Complicated" to something that gives you enjoyable, lasting relationships.

Index

About the Author

Gretchen Anderson consults with clients to inform their product strategy and improve team collaboration skills. She spent the first part of her career in design consulting at firms like frog design, Cooper, and LUNAR. She was Head of Design at PG&E, California's largest energy company; she has led the design of the hardware and software of a next-generation surgical system; and served as VP of Product at GreatSchools.org. Gretchen is a Bay Area native who left only long enough to get a bachelor's degree from Harvard in History & Literature.

Colophon

The cover illustration is by Randy Comer. The cover fonts are Helvetica Condensed and Guardian Sans. The text font is Scala Pro and the heading font is Benton Sans.